Unofficial

DISNEY

Fun & Interesting Facts

from the most engaging

Mulan
Aladdin
Cinderella
Lilo & Stitch
Raya and the Last Dragon
Brother Bear
Zootopia
Tangled
Bolt

to the most elusive facts

UNCOVER
THE SECRETS OF THE
MAGICAL WORLD

Max Galaxy

Copyright © 2024 by Max Galaxy. All rights reserved.

This book and its contents are protected by copyright and other intellectual property laws. No part of this publication may be reproduced or transmitted in any form or by any means, electronic or mechanical, including photocopying, recording, or any information storage and retrieval system, without written permission from the publisher, except for the use of brief quotations in a book review.

This work is created in admiration of Disney and is not an official Disney publication. Trademarks mentioned herein belong to their respective owners and are used for identification purposes only. The author and publisher disclaim any liability for any inaccuracies or omissions.

HOW TO ENJOY THIS BOOK

Welcome to "Disney Fun & Interesting Facts." In this book, you won't find a table of contents because each page is designed to be a surprise, unveiling secrets and stories from the Disney universe in an unexpected sequence.

I've added a mini-game called "Find the Hidden Mickeys". As you explore the facts, keep an eye out for the five elusive Mickey Mouse silhouettes hidden within the pages. Your task is to find all of them, testing your keen observational skills.

Additionally, I've introduced rare and legendary marks to highlight the most exceptional facts. Facts marked as rare are those that were challenging to uncover, even as an avid fan of Disney movies and history. A legendary mark signifies even more extensive research into various sources.

These additions to the guide are designed to enhance your reading experience, inviting you to delve deeper into the magical world of Disney.

Happy hunting!

GATEWAY TO THE DISNEY WORLD

Are you ready for an unforgettable journey?

Dive into this book and take a peek behind the scenes of your favorite Disney cartoons. Learn how artists draw magical worlds, how composers create enchanting melodies, and how characters come to life, bringing us joy and inspiration.

In this book, you will find:

◇ **The secrets of creating cartoons:** How ideas are born, how the animation process goes, and what challenges the creators face along the way.

◇ **The life and legacy of Walt Disney:** Learn how a simple dreamer created an empire that has brought joy to people for many years.

◇ **Fascinating stories:** Funny to inspiring facts that will tell you about the world of Disney from unexpected angles.

◇ **Adorable illustrations:** Immerse yourself in the world of Disney with the help of cute illustrations.

Welcome to a journey through the world of Disney, where every fact and story reveals its magic, lessons about life, friendship, and dreams. I hope this book will make you smile and give you a new perspective on your favorite stories.

P.S. Side effects of reading: uncontrollable desire to rewatch cartoons and an irresistible urge to go to Disneyland. You might even get the exotic idea to try cooking food from Arendelle. :)

FROM SKETCHES TO EMPIRE

1. Walt Disney's Early Journey

Even as a child, Disney wanted to draw, but his father didn't buy him pencils, considering it a silly and useless pursuit. However, this didn't stop the boy. He drew his first picture on the wall of his house with tar. It was a cow. And he received his first fee for a drawing of a horse when the owner of the animal gave the little boy 25 cents for it.

2. Walt Disney's Young Years

When Disney was 16, he ran away from his tyrannical father

to France. It was 1918, the First World War was not over yet, and Walter, having forged a birth certificate and adding a couple of years, got a job as a driver for the Red Cross. He painted the car with pictures, too.

3. The Disney Brothers

Walt created his own animation studio with the money from his brother Roy. And until it started making a profit, he also lived at his expense. Roy even cooked for his younger brother, who was always immersed in work, although he complained about the quality of the food.

> **Funny Fact:** One brother creates Mickey Mouses, the other macaroni and cheese!

4. Disney was laughed at for his plans to release a full-length animated film

When Walt Disney decided to make his first full-length animated film, "Snow White and the Seven Dwarfs," no one really believed in its success. There was no money for the project, and Disney had to mortgage his own house. The film cost $1,488,423 to make, but it easily recouped its money, earning $416 million at the box office. It was after this film that Disney made a bet on full-length films.

Walt Disney and 'Snow White' showed that real magic starts with faith and dreams! ✨

* Rare *

5. Renaming the legend

When Walt Disney told his wife Lillian about the name Mortimer, she decided it didn't match the character's personality.

From Sketches to Empire

Later, Mickey Mouse was invented, and Mortimer became his wise rival, who appeared episodically in short films from 1936 onwards.

Curious: The people who voiced Minnie and Mickey Mouse were married in real life.

6. One actor dubbed the character into different languages for half a century

For over 50 years, Clarence Nash voiced the character. Walt Disney was amazed by the actor's voice and invited him to audition. Indeed, Donald Duck's speech sounds very unusual, and it is almost impossible to completely copy his timbre. That's why Clarence Nash himself dubbed the cartoons featuring his character into other languages. "I learned to quack in French, Spanish, Portuguese, Japanese, German and Chinese," the actor admitted.

Legendary 😍

7. Walt Disney's Favorite Princess 👑

American singer and actress Ilene Woods, who voiced Cinderella, once recalled how old Walt told her: "You're my favorite heroine, you know?" Ilene clarified: "You mean Cinderella?" "Yes," Disney replied, "there's something about that story that's very personal to me."

Curious: The transformation of Cinderella's rags into a ball gown was Walt Disney's favorite animation moment from his film.

"Even miracles take a little time" — Fairy Godmother, "Cinderella"

8. Disney's Dream in 'Sleeping Beauty'

Walt Disney always positioned "Sleeping Beauty" as a film that realized his old dream: the dance in the clouds of the prince and princess. "Love is a flight, so show it here," he told the animators.

9. Which cartoon won its author 8 Oscar statuettes at once?

The Oscar for Best Animated Feature Film was not awarded until 2002. The cartoons "Snow White and the Seven Dwarfs," "Who Framed Roger Rabbit" and "Toy Story" were awarded special prizes. Walt Disney's award for "Snow White" consisted of 8 statuettes at once: one large and seven small ones.

Interesting: During the creation of "Snow White," Walt Disney kept a real zoo of animals in the studio - as a live example for the animators.

The blush on Snow White's face was painted with real blush. At that time, technology could not convey the natural shade, and one of the female animators came up with the idea of using real cosmetics on the drawing.

10. Why do we see the combination A113 in many Pixar and Disney cartoons?

Many students at the California Institute of the Arts studied graphic design and character animation in classroom A113. There is a reference to this combination in all Pixar cartoons and many Disney animated films. For example, it is the car number in the cartoons "Cars," "Toy Story" and "Lilo & Stitch," the model of the camera of the diver from "Finding

Nemo," and the room number in "Monsters University." The autopilot of the spaceship from "WALL-E" received the code A113, which means the directive never to return to Earth.

★ Rare ★

11. Missing Parents: A Recurring Motif in Disney

Executive producer Don Hahn explained this unexpectedly cruel phenomenon with the following words: "Movies are 80 or 90 minutes long, but Disney cartoons are about growing up. They're about that day in your life when you have to take responsibility."

In other words, the animators had to fit the brightest and most important messages of the cartoons into a limited time frame, and what can be more tragic, sad and irreparable in life than the death of a loved one?

12. What is the real secret of Disney cartoons' success?

Disney literally hides either a Mickey Mouse toy or its outline in every new cartoon. For example, in "Zootopia," the toy is hidden in a baby carriage, and in "Frozen," it is hidden on a shelf with dishes. They say this is the secret of the studio's universal love and the commercial success of their cartoons: who knows, maybe it's true?

13. Disney employees used a phrase from "Bambi" in their work

In the cartoon "Bambi," the animals warned each other about the danger with the phrase "Man in the forest." Disney employees began to use this quote in life and with its help notified colleagues about the appearance of Walt Disney in the studio. This moment was even shown in the biographical film "Saving Mr. Banks."

> **Funny Fact:** Time to put down the coffee and pick up the pencils!

14. When Disney characters leave their mark in Hollywood ★

Some Disney characters have been awarded their own stars on the Hollywood Walk of Fame.

On November 18, 1978, Mickey Mouse became not only the first Disney character to receive his own star, but also the first animated character on the Walk of Fame. Since then, six more Disney characters have received stars: Snow White (1987), Kermit the Frog (2002), Donald Duck (2004), Winnie the Pooh (2006), Tinker Bell (2010) and Muppet (2012).

UNVEILING DISNEYLAND'S MAGIC

* Rare *

1. Finding a Home for Mickey

During the 1930s, Disney Studios received many letters from fans asking "Where does Mickey Mouse live?" This inspired Walt to build a small park with statues and rides featuring Mickey and other Disney characters. Although the initial idea was never realized, the concept turned into what eventually became Disneyland.

Curious: In 1933, Mickey Mouse received 800,000 letters from fans.

Funny Fact: It seems Walt Disney decided that the answer to the letters should be big!

2. Doubts and Triumph

No one believed in the success of Disneyland. When Walter was looking for investors, he was rejected 302 times. Even his brother, who always supported him in everything, this time doubted that the venture would pay off.

Disney spent all his money, but made the idea a reality. His park opened in 1955, and within six months, it had been visited by 1 million people.

3. The Story of Magical Inspiration

Did you know that the enchanting Sleeping Beauty Castle in Disneyland has a real twin in Germany?

It's true! The majestic Neuschwanstein Castle, located in the picturesque Bavarian Alps, was the real inspiration for the Disney castle from the fairy tale. The castle, created by King Ludwig II, known as the 'Fairy Tale King', looks like it came straight out of a Disney movie. Today, Neuschwanstein continues to attract crowds of tourists from all over the world, making it one of the most visited places in Germany.

So, next time you're walking around the famous castle in Disneyland, remember it has a cousin located in the Bavarian hills!

★ Rare ★

4. What did the workers put up signs with Latin inscriptions around on the opening day of Disneyland?

By July 17, 1955, when Disneyland officially opened, not all the work had been completed on time. For example, there were many weeds growing on both sides of the canal where the boats for one of the rides traveled.

Instead of weeding in a hurry, Disney ordered the workers to put up signs with exotic plant names in Latin, creating the illusion of a botanical garden.

5. Walt Disney Had a Secret Apartment in Disneyland 🏠

One of the best kept secrets in Disneyland is the existence of Walt's secret apartment, located right in the center. The Disney family would go there when work required it or when they needed to host high-level guests.

To this day, you can notice a lamp turned on in the window of the apartment - it burns day and night to emphasize that the "boss" is still on site.

CINDERELLA

1. Cinderella's Shoe Size is 33.5

Can you imagine how tiny her feet are? It must have been very difficult for her to find shoes that fit, even in a fairy tale world.

> **Funny Fact:** Now it's clear why she lost her shoes so often 😉

2. Cinderella Loses Her Shoes Three Times in the Entire Movie

The first time is when she is serving breakfast to her sisters and stepmother. The second time is when she runs from the

Cinderella ◇ 17

castle at midnight. And the third time is when she runs down the stairs at the wedding.

★ Rare ★

3. The Shoes Became a Symbolic Message

Cinderella is so delicate she can walk in glass slippers without breaking them.

Curious: Like Snow White, Cinderella spends most of her life without a father. Instead, she is under the care of a cruel and envious stepmother. Both heroines were forced to become servants in their own homes.

4. The Battle for the Disney Throne

Cinderella is often considered the main Disney princess. She is often placed in the center of promotional images. This has become a subject of controversy, as she is only the second princess after Snow White. Some believe that Snow White deserves to be the main one because she is the main character of the first Disney animated film, which appeared 13 years before Cinderella. What do you think?

Curious: Cinderella is the only princess who wears a simple maid's outfit in the castle. Other princesses wear royal attire when they are in their kingdom.

5. Maleficent and Cinderella's Stepmother Are the Same Person

But only in real life. Actress Eleanor Audley voiced Lady Tremaine - Cinderella's wicked stepmother - and Maleficent from "Sleeping Beauty."

THE JUNGLE BOOK

1. Bringing the Jungle to Life

"The Jungle Book," premiered on October 18, 1967, at the renowned Grauman's Chinese Theatre in Hollywood, stands as Disney's 19th feature film and the last project overseen by Walt Disney himself. Directed by the veteran Wolfgang Reitherman, a key figure at Disney, the film brought Rudyard Kipling's characters to life with unique and memorable designs, thanks to the collaborative effort of Disney's leading animators. This marked a significant milestone in animation history, showcasing the studio's ability to blend storytelling with artistic innovation.

2. The Story Behind The Jungle Book's Script

Walt Disney, aiming for a lighter tone for "The Jungle Book," diverged from Rudyard Kipling's original, darker narrative. This decision led to a fallout with the initial screenwriter, Bill Peet, resulting in his departure from the project. Larry Clemmons was then brought on board as the new screenwriter, steering the film towards a more family-friendly direction that better aligned with Disney's vision.

3. The Bird Quartet

Originally, the "Singing Vultures" quartet was supposed to be voiced by the members of The Beatles. The artists even specially drew the birds to look like the Liverpool quartet, but something went wrong in the end. Some say that Lennon refused for the whole group, others say they simply could not agree on the schedule.

Legendary

4. From Menace to Mirth

To ensure Kaa the python appeared more comical than menacing, Disney's animators designed him with exaggerated features: a disproportionately large head, a flat nose, and eyes reminiscent of ping-pong balls.

This artistic choice was instrumental in transforming Kaa into a character that, despite his intentions, ended up being more humorous than frightening, aligning with the overall playful and adventurous tone of the movie.

Funny Fact: Disney's animators: 'Let's make Kaa less 'hiss' and more 'haha'!

5. Mowgli and His Wolf Family

Mowgli's wolf family doesn't play a big role in most movies. Most likely, this was done so there were not too many characters in the plot to focus on the main story. However, the wolves are shown to care deeply for him. For example, when Mowgli's brother and sister lick his face to show their affection. Also, when his adoptive father, Rama expressed unwillingness and great sadness when the wolf council decided that Mowgli should return to the people.

The Jungle Book ◇ 21

THE LITTLE MERMAID

1. Ariel Could Have Been Blonde

The audience might never have seen Ariel's iconic red hair. She was originally conceived as a blonde. However, the animators decided she would look too much like the mermaid from the popular movie "Splash,",which had been released a few years before Disney's "The Little Mermaid." Moreover, the red color goes so well with Ariel's emerald tail that we can't imagine her any other way now.

* Rare *

2. Weightless Beauty: A Space-Based Approach to Ariel's Hair

To figure out how Ariel's hair moves underwater, the creators watched the movement of astronauts' hair in zero gravity. That's why there is a "cloud" effect around the mermaid's head.

3. Ariel was drawn in the image and likeness of actress Alyssa Milano

Apparently, the artist and animator Glen Keane was quite taken with either a successful photograph or Alyssa herself. And he decided to express his admiration in this unusual way.

4. From Drawing to Sea Tale

The hand-drawn cartoon "The Little Mermaid" has over 1 million drawings, 1,000 different colors and 1,100 backgrounds. And all this without the help of a computer!

Curious: Ariel became the first Disney princess in 30 years (the cartoon was released in 1989). Before her, this proud title was held by Aurora (Sleeping Beauty, 1959).

5. Epic Storm

It took the animators working on the effects at Disney Studios nearly a year to create the moment when Prince Eric nearly dies during the storm.

After all the titanic work, the scene lasted only two minutes of screen time in the final version of the film. The animators wanted the audience to feel like they were in the storm with Eric as he struggles to survive. And it looks like they succeeded!

> **Funny Fact:** A year of work for two minutes of film? I hope when the final touches were added, one of the animators shouted 'Who ordered the express storm delivery?' 🚀 😄

6. Global Production of "The Little Mermaid"

Every bubble in "The Little Mermaid" is drawn by hand. And there are more than a million of them! To cope with such a volume of work, the studio sent part of its efforts to the Chinese company Pacific Rim Productions. But even this production force was not enough. And in addition to the main animation center in Glendale and an additional one in Beijing, it was necessary to open another one - located outside of Orlando.

Such exorbitant production costs made "The Little Mermaid" one of the studio's most expensive works.

7. The Name of the Crab

The beginning of the movie shows that the crab's full name is Horatio Thelonious Ignacious Crustaceous Sebastian. It is easy to understand why the creators decided to shorten it to just Sebastian.

> **Funny Fact:** When the crab's name sounds like a spell! 😲 👍

★ Rare ★

8. How a Blockbuster Inspired Disney

One of the final scenes of the cartoon, where Ursula significantly increases in size to attack Ariel and Eric, appeared thanks to... the action movie "Die Hard." Disney chairman Jeffrey Katzenberg was very impressed after seeing this film. After that, he visited the studio where the work was in full swing and turned to the directors with an appeal to add "something like that" to the cartoon in preparation.

9. Ariel and Eric's Relationship

Unlike the cartoon, in the 2023 film adaptation, the relationship between the main characters has a stronger foundation than just a fleeting crush. Ariel and Eric find a lot in common. First, both feel suppressed in their families. The mermaid cannot find a common language with her strict father, and the prince - with his stern stepmother.

Second, the characters discover in each other the same passion for collecting all sorts of trinkets and exploring the world around them.

10. Ariel Has Children

Viewers are delighted to watch the events of their favorite cartoons unfold, but sometimes they do not even realize that the cult films about princesses have sequels. Sequels are often released decades after the first story comes out.

Therefore, fans may not know that, for example, the daughter of Ariel and Eric repeated her mother's path and fell into the clutches of an evil sorceress. Fortunately, everything ended well.

THE FLIGHT TO NEVERLAND

1. Delayed Flight to Neverland

Walt Disney was a fan of the story "Peter Pan and Wendy." That's why he decided that he must make a cartoon based on it. Moreover, he planned to start production on the film right after finishing work on the cartoon "Snow White and the 7 Dwarfs," but due to problems with copyright, the process was greatly delayed. As a result, the film was not released until 1952.

2. Roy Disney Was Against "Peter Pan"

The eldest Disney brother had a hard time digesting the news of the $3 million budget, and when the costs rose to $4

million, he probably went into a rage. It all resulted in a big fight between him and Walt. However, in the end, everything worked out: "Pan" grossed over $40 million at the box office during its initial release and another $46.6 million after its re-release in 1980.

3. Peter Pan's Literary Roots

The cartoon "Peter Pan" is not a standalone cartoon. It was based on the book by James Barrie, published in 1911, although there was a play before that, which was staged 7 years before the release of the story.

Curious: The author of Peter Pan, James Barrie, repeatedly changed and revised the work. Originally, the characters in his fairy tale could fly just like that. However, after several cases of children who imitated Peter Pan and fell from beds were injured, Barrie added magic dust as a necessary condition for flight.

4. The True Face of Tinker Bell

Contrary to popular belief, the fairy Tinker Bell from the cartoon "Peter Pan" was not created in the image of Marilyn Monroe. Her prototype was actress and model Margaret Kerry. She even acted out some scenes to give the animators the opportunity to copy her movements.

BEAUTY AND THE BEAST

1. When Beast Met Melody

"Beauty and the Beast" was originally intended to be a darker, more dramatic, and non-musical adaptation. And the action was supposed to take place in 18th century France. However, after watching a 20-minute clip of sketches with temporary vocals that outlined the story, Jeffrey Katzenberg, then chairman of Walt Disney Studios, decided to scrap this version and start over.

2. The Story is Not Entirely Fictional

In the 16th century, Petrus Gonsalvus lived on the island of Tenerife in Spain. He suffered from hypertrichosis. It is a disease that causes excessive hair growth on the face and body. At that time, such a disease was considered "demonic." But with the help of the king, Gonsalvus married a beautiful woman, Catherine, and they had seven children together. It is believed that this story formed the basis of the fairy tale "Beauty and the Beast."

3. Belle and Ballet Harmony 🩰

Belle's movements maintain an atmosphere of elegance. This was at the request of the story writers and producers of "Beauty and the Beast", where they studied the movements of ballerinas during Belle's development. Like ballerinas, Belle walks quickly and diligently on her toes, regardless of what shoes she wears or where she is. She can subconsciously navigate a crowded street while reading, not bumping into other people or objects (though with a few misses), at one point even dodging water.

Curious: Translated from French, Belle's name means "beautiful."

4. An Open Mind in a Closed World

Belle is a smart and intelligent girl who, thanks to her love of reading, has accumulated a significant amount of knowledge, a large vocabulary, a rich imagination and an open mind over the years. She is very outspoken and confident in her beliefs and, therefore, does not like being told what to do. Despite this, Belle does not have many friends. Her intelligence and open mind set her apart from the other villagers, who consider her quite strange.

* Rare *

5. Belle is the Only One in the Entire Village Who Wears Blue

Did you notice that the villagers are dressed in red, yellow, green, and only the young beauty Belle wears a blue dress? By this, the creators of the film emphasize that she is different from everyone else and strives for something more. By the way, the Beast also prefers blue. So, they are really made for each other! ♡

Curious: Belle's hair is always a little disheveled, and one naughty strand always falls on her face. And the writers did this on purpose: by doing so, they emphasized the princess's imperfection and the fact that she looks like an ordinary girl.

6. 👀 Human Eyes in a Beastly Shell

The appearance of the Beast is a whole mixture of wild animals: the mane of a lion, the beard and head of a buffalo, the eyebrows of a gorilla, the tusks of a wild boar, the body of a bear, the legs and tail of a wolf, and only the eyes - of a human.

Legendary

7. The Origin of the Sculptures

Surely everyone remembers those creepy monster figures that decorate the Beast's castle. The sculptures look especially creepy and gloomy at the beginning of the cartoon, when Belle is exploring the castle in fear. As it turned out, most of the sculptures are various early versions of the Beast that were made by artists in the process of creating his image.

8. Jackie Chan Voiced the Beast in the Chinese Version of the Cartoon

In China, the Beast from the cartoon "Beauty and the Beast" spoke with the voice of Hong Kong actor Jackie Chan. The actor also used his musical education, received at the Peking Opera School. In addition to voicing one of the main characters, Jackie Chan performed songs, including the most famous - Beauty and the Beast, which was originally sung by Celine Dion and Peabo Bryson.

9. French Accent

Although the action of the cartoon "Beauty and the Beast" takes place in France, Lumiere is the only one who really speaks with a French accent.

Curious: In the 2017 remake, he is depicted with legs, unlike the original cartoon, where he can only jump on his "stand."

"You have no time to be timid. You must be bold and brave" – Lumiere

THE MAGIC BEHIND ALADDIN

1. Oriental Flair

In "Aladdin," during the song, the Genie mentions taking an order from Aladdin. To maximally match the oriental setting of the cartoon, the animators considered everything to the smallest detail and added an inscription in Persian to the Genie's notebook. It is clearly visible in the frame and means "Plov with turkey." The Genie not only writes in hieroglyphs but also does it from right to left. Such a small detail may go unnoticed on the first viewing.

Curious: Tom Cruise's portrait was used as the basis for Aladdin's face.

* Rare *

2. Applause on Demand: A Funny Moment 🎬

In the cartoon, the "Applause" sign after the Genie's song appeared when producer Jeffrey Katzenberg asked the animators why no one applauded after the songs at the pre-screenings. The animators jokingly drew this sign, and it ended up in the final version.

3. The Fate of the Genie

Little is told about the fate of the Genie in the cartoon. We only know that the main character still granted his friend freedom.

In the film, more attention was paid to this charismatic character. While Aladdin is courting Jasmine, the Genie begins a romantic relationship with the princess's maid, Dalia. In the end, the characters get married and have children. In this version, by the way, the Genie becomes a sailor and travels on a ship with his family.

Legendary 🤩

4. The Genie Sells His Own Lamp

In Aladdin's world, everything is not so simple, especially when it comes to selling magic lamps. But hold on tight because here's a fun and interesting fan theory: the very merchant who offers the lamp is actually... the Genie!

Yes, yes, these two characters have a lot in common: four fingers on each hand (all other characters have a full set on their hands), a unique style with a blue outfit, a red sash, a beard, and the same inimitable voice of Robin Williams. And the main trick up their sleeve (or in their lamp?) is magic. So, if you think the merchant just wants to sell the goods, think again!

5. Unexpected Approach to Voice Acting

The scene at the very beginning of the film, where the street vendor offers the viewer his goods, was created like this: Robin Williams, who voiced the vendor, was brought to the recording studio, where there was a box with various objects covered with a blanket. Then the microphone was turned on, the blanket was removed, and Williams began to describe these objects, which he saw for the first time in his life.

"Imagine that you have three wishes, three hopes, three dreams, and they can all come true." – a beautiful slogan for the cartoon Aladdin.

6. The Ups and Downs of Robin Williams' Relationship with Disney

Robin Williams agreed to voice the Genie for a significantly reduced fee because he wanted to do it for his children. The only thing he asked was that his voice not be used for merchandise. Disney agreed, but then realized that the Genie had really become the star of the film and used the actor's voice for merchandise anyway. This caused a big scandal between Robin and Disney. To make amends, Disney sent Williams a Picasso painting worth over $1 million. They eventually made up.

Curious: Robin Williams received four awards for his performance as the Genie.

7. Jasmine Speaks and Sings with Different Voices

Princess Jasmine was voiced by actress Linda Larkin. However, in the memorable duet with Aladdin, it is not her voice that sounds, but that of the singer Lea Salonga. She also sang for Mulan later.

There is an opinion that Larkin did not dare to perform Jasmine's part, believing her voice was not very suitable for the princess.

8. It's immediately clear that Jasmine liked Aladdin, as evidenced by the flower

Throughout the cartoon, we can see the flower that Aladdin gives to his beloved in her hair, and then on the princess's table. The creators of the film emphasize that Jasmine liked this gift, as it reminded her of Aladdin, so the girl decided to keep it.

9. Laughter, Chaos, and True Friendship

The little pocket monkey named Abu, who is virtually voiceless, plays an important role in the cartoon. He repeatedly helps out his friend, though he just as often gets him into big trouble, such as the collapse of the Cave of Wonders and involuntary imprisonment.

However, despite everything, this character pleases the audience with his serenity, kindness, sometimes amuses with his cunning, ingenuity, sometimes greed and even jealousy.

Funny Fact: Abu may not speak, but his facial expressions are worth a thousand words. Especially when it comes to 'Oops, we're kind of in trouble again'.

"Why, you hairy little thief." - Aladdin to Abu

The Magic Behind Aladdin ◇ 37

THE LION KING'S WORLD

1. Success Story Against All Odds

Not everyone believed in the success of "The Lion King." Many studio employees doubted that the story of a young lion framed for his father's murder by his uncle, set to music by Elton John, would appeal to audiences. Even the screenwriters were skeptical: Brenda Chapman didn't want to take on the job because "the story wasn't very good," and writer Burny Mattinson said, "I don't know who's going to watch it."

2. A Shadow Project Becomes a Legend

"The Lion King" was considered a secondary project - all the studio's bets were placed on "Pocahontas." Well, the pessimistic predictions of the skeptics were not to be fulfilled, and "The Lion King" became one of the most successful animations in world history, which also marked the renaissance of Disney animation in the early 1990s. And yes, compare the total box office collections of "The Lion King" and "Pocahontas": $968 million vs. $346 million.

* Rare *

3. Evolution of the Title of Everyone's Favorite Cartoon

Among the working titles of the cartoon was "The King of Beasts," but later, it was decided to call the picture "The King of the Jungle." However, the creators soon remembered that lions do not live in the jungle, and as a result, the cartoon was given the title "The Lion King."

By the way, they say that in Disneylands, you can find T-shirts with the original title "The King of the Jungle": maybe one of the readers has one? 🐻

4. From Shakespeare to the Savannah

The creators have repeatedly stated that the inspiration for the story of "The Lion King" was Shakespeare's "Hamlet" and the biblical stories of Joseph and Moses. By the way, there is a scene in the cartoon where Scar plays with a skull - a kind of reference by the authors to "Hamlet."

5. Reflection of a Legend

The plot and artistic techniques of "Bambi" had a significant influence on another popular Disney cartoon - "The Lion King." For example, both cartoons begin with the birth of the main character. In both cartoons, the main character loses a parent, and both cartoons end with a strong fire and subsequent rebirth of nature, and one of the symbols of both cartoons is the main character standing on top of a cliff. Even the creators of "The Lion King" do not deny the significant influence of "Bambi" on their creation.

Curious: Bambi is similar to Simba: as a child, as they grew older, both tried to become brave, learned life lessons, and in their youth fell in love with their childhood friends.

6. Pumbaa Breaks Disney Taboos

Pumbaa is the first Disney character in history to fart. 😄 Before that, no cartoon character had ever allowed themselves to do such a thing!

> **Funny Fact:** Pumbaa proved there is a place for naturalness in the Disney world. And this place sounds louder than ever! 😊

"Hakuna Matata" — Timon and Pumbaa

Rare

7. Lions? Nope, That Roar is All Human

The epic lion roars in "The Lion King"? They're not real lions! It's actually a guy named Frank Welker making those sounds. The filmmakers wanted each lion to have a unique and powerful roar, and Frank nailed it.

Curious: Disney actually got sued after the movie came out... by hyena researchers! They felt the movie made hyenas look like total bad guys.

8. Scar's Claws as a Sign of His Character

The villain Scar is the only lion whose claws are visible in every scene he appears in. This probably indicates his readiness to always attack his enemies and defeat them.

9. Scarface: Jungle Edition

Ever notice how Scar's face looks a lot like a certain famous movie gangster? His scar is almost identical to Tony Montana's (Al Pacino) in the movie "Scarface."

10. Mufasa & Scar: Not Actually Brothers?!

It turned out that the creators were hiding an interesting detail: according to the authors, Mufasa and Scar are not brothers, but rather two lions living in the same pride. The directors claim that in the wild, when the leader gets old, a stronger and younger lion appears, and they wanted to use facts from animal life. At that moment, they realized that Mufasa and Scar could not be brothers, but for some reason, they did not tell the audience about it for many years.

So now, that same scene in the gorge doesn't seem so tragic

anymore, though it's still very painful to watch.

11. When Nature Becomes Animation

Remember that iconic cliff where Simba gets presented as a cub? It's based on a real place! You can find a similar rock formation in Hell's Gate National Park in Kenya.

12. What's in a Name? Swahili Secrets!

Most of the names in "The Lion King" actually come from the Swahili language!

- ◇ Simba = Lion
- ◇ Rafiki = Friend
- ◇ Pumbaa = Simpleton
- ◇ Shenzi = Savage

Curious: Keep an eye on Simba as a cub. Sometimes, his whiskers magically appear and disappear! Oops!

POCAHONTAS

1. Bringing 'Pocahontas' to Life

The 'Pocahontas' movie premiere on June 23, 1995, was intentionally set to honor the 400th birthday of the real Pocahontas.

This film brings to life the story of Pocahontas, also known as Matoaka, highlighting her adventures and heritage. It's a special way to celebrate her legacy and make her story known to a new generation.

Curious:

⋄ To authentically depict the setting, the film's crew visited Virginia, capturing the essence of its landscapes and wildlife.

⋄ Throughout production, Disney consulted with Native American scholars and community members to accurately represent their culture and traditions.

⋄ Glen Keane, a legendary animator who contributed to characters like Aladdin and Ariel, led the design for Pocahontas, adding to the film's historical and cultural depth.

2. Pocahontas' Wardrobe: One Dress for All Occasions

Talk about a fashionista! Pocahontas is the only Disney princess who doesn't change her outfit throughout the entire movie. That's right, she rocks the same dress from beginning to end. And get this: her color choice is totally different from other princesses. While they're all about that blue, Pocahontas goes for a shade that complements her complexion.

Curious: Pocahontas also made history as the first Disney princess with a visible tattoo!

"Sometimes, the right path is not the easiest one." – Grandmother Willow

★ Rare ★

3. The Story That Changed 'Pocahontas'

In Disney's animated film, the character of Grandmother Willow was originally conceived as a male spirit of the river, named "Old Man River." This role was even offered to actor Gregory Peck. However, Peck suggested that the film would benefit more from a maternal figure.

BOOM! Grandmother Willow was born, and she's now one of the best parts of the story, guiding Pocahontas with her wisdom and love for nature.

4. A 🐀 Reveals a Character's True Colors

Here's a sneaky detail you might have missed: when Governor Ratcliffe is boarding the ship, there's a rat in the foreground doing the same thing. This subtle moment actually hints at the character's greedy and selfish nature.

FROM MYTH TO SCREEN: HERCULES

1. Hercules is 18 years old

This detail comes from the myth that inspired the movie. The Fates predicted that Hades would gain power after 18 years. The only one who could stop him was Zeus' son, Hercules, who would be old enough to fight evil by then.

"I'm on my way. I can go the distance. No matter how far. Somehow, I'll find the strength. I know every mile will be worth my while. I would go most anywhere to find my place."
- Hercules

2. Hercules is Ariel's cousin

Think about it. Ariel is Triton's daughter. Triton is Poseidon's son. Poseidon is Zeus' brother. And Zeus is Hercules' father.

> **Funny Fact:** Imagine the family reunions!

3. A celestial event with a limitation

There's an interesting detail where the Fates tell Hades about a prophecy, which includes a celestial event where six planets align. This scene accurately reflects the knowledge of the ancient Greeks, who were aware of only five planets besides Earth, visible to the naked eye. These planets were Mercury, Venus, Mars, Jupiter, and Saturn.

The inclusion of six planets in the film's portrayal of the planetary alignment is a nod to historical accuracy, with Earth being the sixth planet known to the ancients. This detail shows Disney's commitment to incorporating scientific and historical facts into their storytelling.

4. Hades gives viewers a clue

At the 46-minute mark, the Lord of the Underworld says, "Relax, folks. We're only halfway there." And 46 minutes is exactly halfway through the 92-minute movie.

> **Funny Fact:** Leave the watch at home! When Hades is on the screen, he not only controls the underworld 😬

From Myth to Screen: Hercules ◇ 47

5. A Rational Villain in a Disney World

Hades, the antagonist in Disney's "Hercules," is a unique character in the Disney villain roster. Unlike many Disney villains who are often portrayed as irrational or purely evil, Hades is depicted as cunning, articulate, and rational, albeit highly temperamental. His motivations stem from jealousy and a desire for power, as he feels sidelined in the Underworld while other gods enjoy the luxuries of Mount Olympus. This portrayal of Hades deviates from the traditional depiction of villains in Disney movies, offering a more complex character.

Curious: Hades is considered one of the funniest villains, alongside Captain Hook, Madam Mim, Pete, Yzma, and Prince John.

Legendary 🤩

6. The Herculean Task of Bringing Hydra to Life

The animation of the Hydra was a remarkable feat, representing a significant challenge for the animators.

This mythological creature, which was fully computer-animated within a traditionally animated film, transformed from a single-headed beast into a multi-headed monster, reaching up to 30 heads.

The complexity of this animation was such that it took the animators between 6 to 14 hours to complete just one frame, depending on the number of heads in the scene. This painstaking process meant that animating the entire four-minute action scene with the Hydra took over a year to complete.

Rare

7. Crafting Pegasus in Disney's Hercules

Zeus makes Hercules' winged-horse companion, Pegasus, out of clouds, and as he does this, he mentions each cloud Zeus creates Pegasus from clouds as a gift for his son. This scene references Nephele, a nymph born from clouds in Greek mythology and cleverly integrates this mythological element. This attention to detail in the film showcases Disney's creative approach to blending mythology with animated storytelling.

8. Hercules' Lion King Connection

In "Hercules," a Disney animated movie, there's a subtle but interesting reference to "The Lion King." In one of the scenes, Hercules is seen wearing a lion skin, which is actually the skin of Scar, the antagonist from "The Lion King."

Additionally, "Hercules" features another amusing nod to popular culture with the "Air Herc" sandals, a clear reference to Nike's "Air" line of shoes, notably the Air Jordan series by basketball player Michael Jordan. Interestingly, the Nike company itself is named after the Greek goddess of victory, tying back to the film's Greek mythology theme.

> **Funny Fact:** I wonder if Nike considered a Hercules line: 'Air Hercs - for when you gotta outrun a Cyclops.

9. Farming, Force, and Fathers

In Disney's "Hercules," there are notable similarities to the original "Star Wars" trilogy. Both Hercules and Luke Skywalker grew up with adoptive farmer parents and later discover their extraordinary powers. Their journeys involve training by smaller mentors - Hercules with Phil and Luke with Yoda - each mentor being persuaded to train their respective students. Additionally, both protagonists learn their fathers are influential figures: Hercules is the son of Zeus, King of the Gods, while Luke's father is the Sith Lord, Darth Vader. Though luckily for Hercules, Zeus isn't evil like Darth Vader.

If you enjoyed discovering the fascinating parallels between Disney's "Hercules" and the "Star Wars" trilogy in this book, you might also be interested in exploring more intriguing facts about the "Star Wars" universe. For more insights into this iconic saga, check out my second book, filled with captivating "Star Wars" facts and trivia, available on Amazon.

10. Decoding the Divine Guests in Hercules

The party thrown by Zeus and Hera on Mount Olympus to celebrate Hercules' birth is graced with the presence of various well-known gods and goddesses. Among them, Hermes is depicted delivering a gift to Zeus, adorned with his iconic winged cap and sandals. Narcissus also makes a cameo, indulging in his self-love by gazing into a mirror.

In the background, several other gods and goddesses can be spotted, each characterized by distinct features. A goddess with heart-shaped hair and a heart clip, resembling Aphrodite, and a god armed with a helmet and sword, suggesting Ares, are notable examples. Poseidon, with a fin and trident, and Athena, holding an owl, also appear, adding depth to the scene with these symbolic representations.

Rare

11. Ancient City, Modern Vibes

The portrayal of Thebes draws amusing parallels to New York City. Phil refers to Thebes as "the Big Olive," humorously playing on New York's nickname "the Big Apple." This comparison extends to Phil's line, "If you can make it there, you can make it anywhere," echoing the famous Frank Sinatra song "New York, New York." These references are part of Disney's tradition of incorporating clever, jokes into their films, adding layers of humor that can be appreciated by audiences of all ages.

12. Emergency Calls in Ancient Greece

There's a clever joke where the henchmen Pain and Panic, disguised as young boys, cry out "Somebody call IX-I-I!" during a scene where they pretend to be trapped under a rock. This line is a witty adaptation of the emergency number 911, using Roman numerals IX-I-I to fit the ancient Greek setting of the movie.

> **Funny Fact:** Imagine dialing IX-I-I in Ancient Greece, and a Minotaur answers: "Is it urgent, or are you just another traveler lost in my maze?"

13. Cupid Strikes! (Literally) 🏹

In Disney's "Hercules," there's a charming detail where Meg gets poked in the back by Cupid's arrow as she's falling in love with Hercules. This moment is a symbolic yet humorous touch, reflecting the theme of love developing between the characters. The inclusion of Cupid's arrow, a well-known symbol associated with love and affection, adds a layer of mythological reference and playful humor to the scene.

From Myth to Screen: Hercules ◇ 51

CRAFTING MULAN'S STORY

1. Music as a Storytelling Tool

The music in "Mulan" plays a special role. Notice how it's vibrant only in the first half of the movie, until the characters reach the destroyed village? After that, the music becomes faint or almost disappears. This was a deliberate directorial choice to create a more tragic and serious atmosphere.

2. Mulan's Floral Identity

The magnolias serve a deeper purpose than mere aesthetic enhancement. These flowers, most notably seen in Mulan's hair comb, are a subtle reference to her name. In Chinese, "Mulan" translates to "wood orchid" or "magnolia," making these flowers a meaningful part of the film's visual storytelling. The animators also intentionally incorporated magnolias, beautifully blending her character with the visual elements of the film.

3. Eyelashes as a Storytelling Device

At the beginning of the movie, Mulan has long eyelashes - a technique illustrators commonly use to depict female characters. But when she disguises herself as a man, her long eyelashes suddenly disappear. Later, when her true identity is revealed, her eyelashes return.

4. How Mushu Challenged Dragon Stereotypes

Legendary 🤩

Creation was a significant departure from typical dragon depictions. Concerned about the traditional portrayal of dragons as intimidating, animators initially shied away from this concept. However, they were inspired by the versatility of dragons in Chinese mythology, as explained by writer Robert D. San Souci. This led to the conception of Mushu as a smaller, more comic figure. Eddie Murphy brought Mushu to life in his first voice-acting role, which paved the way for his later success as Donkey in "Shrek."

5. Shan Yu's Hidden Skill

For most of the film, Shan Yu holds his sword in his bare right hand. However, for a brief moment during the chase scene, when he breaks through the door and just before he cuts the first wooden pillar, he holds the sword in his gloved left hand before switching back to his right. This could mean he is ambidextrous - someone who can use both hands equally well.

Curious: Shan Yu probably has the highest onscreen kill count of any Disney villain.

6. A New Twist for the Villain

The creators took a creative approach to the villain Shan Yu's ending, avoiding the cliche of him falling off a cliff like many Disney villains. Instead, they crafted a dramatic and memorable scene on the palace roof where Mulan uses her resourcefulness and teamwork with Mushu to launch fireworks, leading to Shan Yu's explosive demise. This unconventional approach to defeating the villain highlights the film's uniqueness and innovation, making the plot more unpredictable.

Curious: He is one of the few Disney villains who doesn't sing and doesn't have a musical number. However, he has a recurring instrumental theme that plays throughout his appearances in the film.

CREATING THE JUNGLE: TARZAN

1. In Search of Inspiration: A Journey to Africa

To create a maximally realistic world for "Tarzan," the Disney animation team embarked on a two-week journey to Africa:

Amboseli National Park (Kenya): Artists sketched the savannah, elephants, lions, giraffes, and other animals. These sketches formed the basis for the backgrounds and character animation.

Bwindi Impenetrable Forest (Uganda): The team observed gorillas in their natural habitat.

Curious: Get this — Tarzan and Jane were actually drawn on opposite sides of the world! Glen Keane worked on Tarzan in Paris, while a whole team in California animated Jane.

* Rare *

2. Jungle on Wheels

To see how Tarzan's body would move while sliding on a log, the animators based his movement on the role of professional skateboarder Tony Hawk when he was on his skateboard.

Curious: Animator Glen Keane's son was very passionate about surfing and skateboarding, which inspired him to incorporate these movements into Tarzan's movements.

> **Funny Fact:** When you have such a famous skateboarding coach, you don't even notice you're sliding on a log in the jungle and not on a ramp.

3. From Lab to Vines 💪

Disney animators hired a professor of anatomy to consult with them on Tarzan's musculature. He superimposed the correct muscle types on their drawings to help them show how to depict a person at the peak of his physical fitness.

Curious: Tarzan bears a striking resemblance to his late father, albeit without a beard and with longer hair. He also inherited his mother's hair and eyes.

4. Tarzan and the Play of Shadows: Light as a Symbol in the Confrontation with Sabor

According to the animators' commentary, the lighting in the Tarzan vs. Sabor duel is symbolic. Whenever Tarzan is safe from Sabor, he is always in the shadows, but he is vulnerable to Sabor when he is out of the shadows.

Curious: Tarzan's name actually means "White Skin" in ape-speak (from the original books).

ATLANTIS: THE LOST EMPIRE

1. Less Singing, More Explosions

After the release of "The Hunchback of Notre Dame," The Walt Disney Company decided they didn't want to make another musical. Instead, they created an action-adventure animated film inspired by the science fiction novels of French author Jules Verne.

Curious: The production crew even wore t-shirts with the slogan "Atlantis - Fewer songs, more explosions" because the movie was planned as an action-adventure.

> **Funny Fact:** Looks like Disney composers had an easy job with 'Atlantis' — the soundtrack is just 'bang,' 'pow,' and 'kaboom'!

2. Bringing Atlantis to Life

Mike Mignola (famous for drawing Hellboy!) gave Atlantis its edgy, graphic look. The characters were all angles – nothing like your typical Disney style. The team didn't just copy ancient Greece for Atlantis either. They studied cultures from India to Tibet and even looked at Plato's descriptions of the city.

Curious: To create interesting locations, the team visited early 20th-century military facilities and explored caves in Karlovy Vary and New Mexico, adding realism and authenticity to the film.

3. Creating the Atlantean Language for Disney

Marc Okrand, known for creating the Klingon language for the "Star Trek" film series, was brought in by Disney to develop the Atlantean language. Okrand, with his extensive experience in creating fictional languages and interest in linguistics, approached the task with great care.

He based it on the Indo-European language family, created a grammar and a concise dictionary of the Atlantean language.

He even chose boustrophedon as their writing style. That means you read one line left-to-right, the next one right-to-left – total brain twister! Marc made hundreds of random sketches of individual writing examples, from which the cartoon creators chose the best.

A group of internet users (The Atlantean Language Group) studied the Atlantean language for a long time despite the lack of publications from the author himself. They developed a grammar and a concise dictionary of this language.

Curious: According to the film's creators, "Atlantean" was the first language in human history, from which all others originated.

> **Funny Fact:** Imagine trying to read the news in Atlantean – you'd need to be a yoga master just to follow the lines!

4. The Science of Survival: Crafting Atlantis's Underwater Ecosystem

The filmmakers crafted a detailed Atlantean ecosystem to explain how the mythical city could thrive underwater. The design centered around the Atlantean crystal, which had the unique ability to draw water up from the ocean. This water, combined with steam generated by the Earth's core magma, was used to irrigate plants, thereby producing oxygen for the city. This innovative concept provided a plausible explanation for the city's survival and sustainability under the sea.

5. Monster Parade 👾

Rare

In the initial stages, the creative team envisioned a plethora of monsters the characters would encounter on their journey to Atlantis. These ideas included various creatures such as Squid Bats, Lava Whales, and a giant creature called the Land Beast. The concept was so extensive that Mike Mignola, who was involved in the film's production, described it as a "monster parade." However, as development progressed, it became clear that including all these creatures would not fit well with the film's narrative. The focus shifted towards developing the bond between Milo and the rest of the crew, leading to a reduction in the number of monsters featured in the final film.

6. Atlantis: Disney's Deadliest Movie?

Atlantis: The Lost Empire is often regarded as one of the more mature films in Disney's animated repertoire, with themes and storytelling designed for an older audience. Notably, it is estimated to have the highest count of implied casualties in any Disney animated movie.

This is primarily due to a significant event in the film's opening, where the sinking of Atlantis, triggered by a volcanic eruption, suggests an estimated 35,000 casualties. Additionally, the final confrontation in the movie accounts for 14 more, including the Atlantean King. This high number is unique, especially compared to other Disney movies known for their dramatic scenes.

7. A Name Inspired by a Volcanic Legend

In the movie, explosives expert Vincenzo "Vinny" Santorini has a last name that's directly connected to his profession. Santorini is a Greek island known for one of the largest volcanic eruptions in history, the Minoan eruption. This event is also linked to the legend of Atlantis, which gives the character's name extra meaning and depth.

8. Why is Atlantis: The Lost Empire a Top 250 Animated Film?

This movie may not be the first one that comes to mind when you think of Disney, but it still holds a special place in the hearts of many 2D animation lovers (including me!). Here are a few reasons why it won over audiences:

⋄ **The Lost City of Atlantis:** This theme has always been fascinating not only to conspiracy theorists but also to anyone who loves stories about ancient civilizations, mysteries, and myths. The movie offers its own interpretation of this legend. We can dive into a world of puzzles, secrets, and adventures (this alone would be enough for me, but it's just one of many reasons).

⋄ **Unique Visual Style:** The movie stands out for its unique visual style, which combines comic book elements with a sci-fi aesthetic. 350 animators and artists worked on the film, which emphasizes the scale and complexity of the project.

⋄ **James Newton Howard:** The movie's composer is James Newton Howard, an eight-time Oscar nominee. His musical contribution to the project was an important part of creating the film's atmosphere. (Of course, I was joking in the first fact that the soundtrack only consists of "bang," "pow" and "kaboom" - its score is really awesome!).

Feel free to add your own reasons to the list in the book's review!

LILO & STITCH

1. The Unique Setting of 'Lilo & Stitch'

"Lilo & Stitch" distinguished itself as Disney's inaugural animated feature film to take place in the modern era and in the picturesque setting of Hawaii. This choice showcased Hawaii's rich culture and its stunning landscapes.

Curious: Adding to the unique charm of "Lilo & Stitch," the film's soundtracks is an eclectic mix of Hawaiian melodies and classic Elvis Presley hits. This combination not only enhances the film's appeal but also beautifully complements its Hawaiian setting.

2. All for the Sake of Beauty

"Lilo & Stitch" was the first Disney film since "Dumbo" (way back in 1941) to use watercolor backgrounds. This gave the picture a look more reminiscent of light book illustrations, creating a warmer and even somewhat old-fashioned atmosphere, in contrast to the more modern-looking films of the studio at that time. By the way, a plush Dumbo can be seen in Lilo's room.

In addition, most of the sequels retained this feature of the original cartoon.

Curious: While watching, you may subconsciously experience a sense of nostalgia for the studio's older film, because the design of most of the episodic aliens here was inspired by the characters of Disney's "Winnie the Pooh."

The film also features other non-standard solutions - for example, the use of real footage from a live-action film in the scene where Stitch sees a movie about a city-destroying monster spider on TV. Or the photographs of Elvis Presley, which Lilo admired so much.

3. Aloha Vibes

To capture the spirit of the Hawaiian islands as accurately as possible, actors Tia Carrere and Jason Scott Lee, who voiced Nani and David and are familiar with the local lifestyle, were brought in to help the writers. They helped rewrite the dialogue of the Hawaiian characters to make it sound natural. Thanks to their input, the original film features real-life local dialect and characteristic Hawaiian slang.

Curious: The name "Lilo" translates from Hawaiian as "Lost." This beautifully resonates with the themes of the film itself - let's remember the scene where Stitch reads about a lost duckling and waits to be found. "Nani" translates as "Beautiful."

Legendary 🤩

4. Let's Talk About the Plot

Not many people know that the original plot of "Lilo & Stitch" was supposed to be completely different. The idea was for Stitch to be an interstellar gangster who, during one of his raids, abandoned a member of his gang, Jumba. Throughout the film, Jumba would have been trying to get revenge on his former leader, and the climax in the third act would have been the arrival of the old team on Earth in search of Stitch.

> **Funny Fact:** Imagine a Star Wars-style battle, but instead of lightsabers, we've got Hawaiian leis and ukuleles. 'The Force' meets 'Aloha'!

5. Disney Multiverse

"Lilo & Stitch" had a rather interesting advertising campaign. For example, four short teaser trailers were released, in which Stitch spoiled iconic scenes from such cartoons as "Aladdin," "Beauty and the Beast," "The Lion King," and "The Little Mermaid" with his presence.

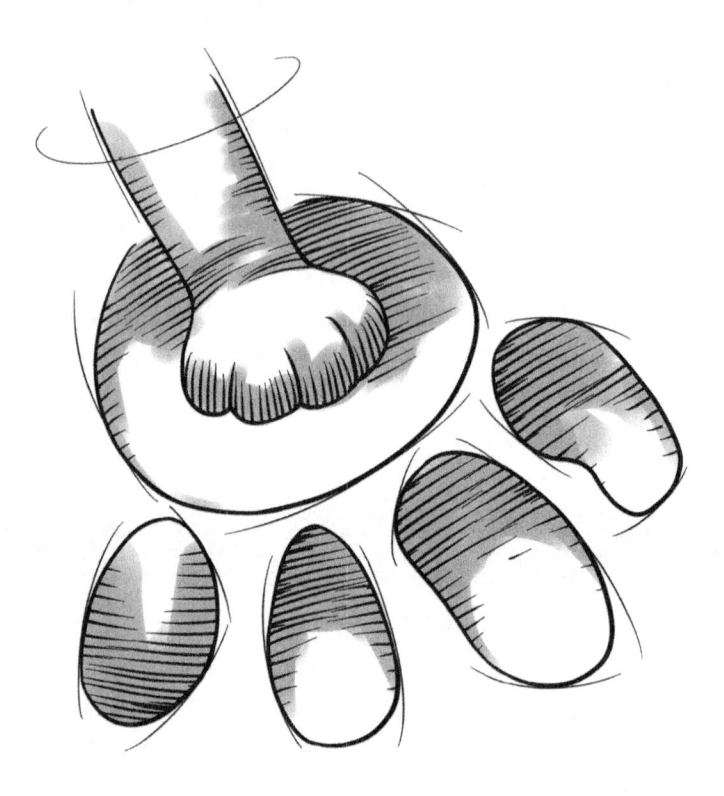

By the way, the original actors were brought back to voice their characters again. Some of them were very surprised that their characters in the commercials were quite negative towards Stitch.

The teaser trailers were called "Inter-Stitch-als" and were included on the DVD release of the cartoon as bonus materials.

Funny Fact: Imagine the surprise of those Disney characters when Stitch showed up uninvited! It's like having an unexpected guest at a party who ends up being the life of it. Stitch, the ultimate party crasher.

6. Sisters, Not Mom & Daughter

In test screenings, many viewers assumed that Nani was Lilo's mother, despite the film repeatedly mentioning that she was her older sister and that their parents were deceased.

To minimize this confusion, a scene was added to the final cut of the film, where the sisters talk about their family, with Lilo saying the word "sisters" three times in a row.

Rare

7. Stitch's Origins

Chris Sanders, one of the two directors of "Lilo & Stitch" (the other was his longtime partner Dean DeBlois), also co-wrote the screenplay, designed the characters, and... voiced Stitch himself. He also said that he came up with the idea for Stitch back in 1985 when he was sketching ideas for a comic book.

Curious: Animating Stitch on screen was quite a challenge. The character has no pupils at all, which makes it very difficult to convey his emotions. The creators tried to compensate for this with very expressive movements and gestures.

And the character's wild popularity is further proof that it all worked out!

8. Subtle Tributes to an Earlier Disney Classic

It's not hard to guess that the creators of the 1998 film "Mulan" also worked on this film. There is a poster of that film in Nani's bedroom, a restaurant called "Mulan Wok" and a poster in the dog shelter with a dog that resembles Little Brother.

Curious: In the scene where the aliens are calculating

Stitch's landing trajectory, the code name for Earth is Area 51.

9. Budget-Friendly Animation

* Rare *

The animation team found creative ways to save on production costs. Not using CGI was one of the primary strategies. They simplified character designs by removing small details like pockets from clothing. To avoid animating complex shadows, which can be costly, many scenes were set in shaded areas, with shadows used only in pivotal scenes.

This approach helped manage the film's budget effectively while maintaining Disney's renowned animation quality.

10. Spaceships Go Undercover (as Sea Creatures)

Forget those boring UFOs! The design of the spaceships and other extraterrestrial elements was inspired by marine life. This unique approach included creating spacecraft that resembled whales, crabs, and other sea creatures, adding an interesting twist to the typical portrayal of alien technology.

The choice to draw inspiration from oceanic forms lends a distinct and imaginative flair to the film's portrayal of outer space, seamlessly blending the unfamiliar and the familiar.

> **Funny Fact:** Why travel in a boring old spaceship when you can cruise the cosmos in a whale-mobile?

11. Stitch the Star Wars Fanboy?

After Stitch's crash landing on Earth, he utters a phrase in his alien language, including the word "Chewbacca." Chewbacca, a beloved character from Star Wars, is known as Han Solo's loyal companion.

This playfully hints at a shared universe between the two films. It's fun to imagine a galaxy where Stitch and Chewbacca might cross paths, perhaps striking up an interstellar friendship.

12. The Art of Hidden Mickeys

Keep an eye out for hidden Mickey Mouse shapes, a classic Easter egg in many Disney films. Animators cleverly incorporated tiny Mickeys into various scenes. Notably, while Lilo is in the shed repairing her doll, a Mickey shape can be spotted on a boot's underside. Additionally, at the market, an arrangement of three fruits subtly forms Mickey's iconic silhouette. These hidden details add a layer of fun for eagle-eyed viewers, offering a playful nod to Disney's beloved mascot.

> **Funny Fact:** Every time I spot a hidden Mickey in Disney movies, I feel like I've joined an exclusive Disney club. It's like a wink from the animators!

13. Stitch's Secret Signature

In the opening scene of "Lilo & Stitch," during Stitch's trial, a councilwoman asks him for a sign of understanding. Stitch humorously responds by licking the interior of his glass containment, leaving a trail of saliva. Interestingly, this trail of saliva forms the iconic 'D' shape, reminiscent of the famous Walt Disney logo.

14. Family Tragedy 😕

Subtle hints about Lilo and Nani's life before their parents' death are gently woven into the narrative. For example, Lilo's peculiar behavior, such as feeding her fish Pudge because he "controls the weather" reflects her coping mechanism after the tragic loss of her parents in a car accident. This ritual symbolizes her desire to control the elements of nature to prevent similar tragedies.

Additionally, Nani's room, adorned with surfing medals and trophies, offers a glimpse into their happier past, highlighting how profoundly their parents' passing has impacted their current lives. This movie has way more depth than you might think at first.

15. The Hawaiian Word that Guarded Lilo's Room

On Lilo's bedroom door is a sign with the word "kapu," a Hawaiian term rooted in other Polynesian languages like Fijian "tabu," from which the English "taboo" derives. Kapu generally translates to "keep out." This detail adds authenticity to the Hawaiian setting of the film. It's interesting to note that many viewers, myself included, may have watched the movie without knowing the meaning of "kapu." Now, understanding it as "keep out" adds a new layer of meaning to the scene.

It's a fun little detail that brings a smile, especially thinking back to how cool it would have been to have "kapu" on my own bedroom door as a kid, embracing the spirit of Lilo's personal space!

16. A Classic Touch

The book "The Ugly Duckling" that Lilo and Stitch read features illustrations from an old Disney adaptation of the story. This adds a touch of nostalgia and history to the scene, connecting it to Disney's long legacy of storytelling.

★ Rare ★

17. The Humor of Sight 👽

In "Lilo & Stitch," there is a humorous detail involving Pleakley, an alien and Jumba's companion. Pleakley often uses a View-Master, a device designed to create a 3D viewing experience by presenting slightly different images to each eye. However, the joke is that Pleakley, having only one eye, wouldn't be able to experience the View-Master's 3D effect. Despite this, Pleakley amusingly continues to use the device, unaware that he's missing out on its intended visual impact. This small, clever gag adds a layer of humor to Pleakley's character and his attempts to understand Earth.

> **Funny Fact:** Pleakley's attempt to use the View-Master always cracks me up. It's like trying to whistle with a mouthful of crackers. Or like watching someone trying to read a book upside down and still nodding along. I got a love of his optimism, though! 😄

18. Stitch's Asian Adventure

While Stitch is beloved around the world, he has found particular popularity in Asia. In countries like China and Japan, you can find a wide range of merchandise featuring the character. Additionally, animated series have been created specifically for Asian audiences, with Stitch's adventures taking place in various locations across the continent.

Lilo & Stitch ◊ 71

THE MAP TO TREASURE PLANET

1. Dream Team, Dream Delayed

The story behind this animated film is a fascinating journey of ideas and technology. In 1985, talented directors Ron Clements and John Musker, known for their work on "The Great Mouse Detective," pitched a unique project: "Treasure Island in Space." However, Jeffrey Katzenberg, a high-ranking Disney executive, rejected the idea, preferring to focus on "The Little Mermaid" instead. This decision led Clements and Musker to create masterpieces like "Aladdin" and "Hercules." They agreed to work on "Hercules" only on the condition that their "Treasure Island" project would eventually be greenlit.

Time showed that the delay in making "Treasure Planet" actually benefited the film. The directors initially wanted to constantly rotate the camera around the characters, inspired by James Cameron and Steven Spielberg, but the animation technology of the time didn't allow for it.

Production on the film finally began in 2000. A team of 350 artists and animators worked on it, growing to over 1,000 people by 2002.

2. Space Adventures with a Classic Twist

During the creation of the film, Disney decided to move away from the traditional representations of spaceships we often see in science fiction and television. Instead of standard metal rockets and spacecraft, all the ships in the film were designed in a classic style reminiscent of pirate ships. This choice of style was not accidental: it is a tribute to the inspiration for the story - classic tales of seafaring adventures. The creators aimed to attract modern children to the exciting adventures of treasure hunting, which might encourage them to read the original book.

Another remarkable feature of the "Treasure Planet" world is Etherium, a space environment, where life is possible without spacesuits. The creators didn't want to depict space as a dark, cold, and dangerous place where every moment could be the last due to a lack of air. Instead, they wanted to show it as a bright, cozy, and welcoming space with air between the planets. This allows travelers to cover vast distances in space without fear of suffocating. Disney's unique approach to depicting space makes "Treasure Planet" a unique and memorable film.

> **Funny Fact:** Imagine the space pirates' surprise when they first learn about space speeds! "So, we don't have to wait for a fair wind to move anymore?" - "No, captain, now we have a hyperdrive!" - "Hyper-what? Order that hyperdrive to raise the sails! 🚀"

3. A Visual Revolution

"Treasure Planet" took animation to the next level with a groundbreaking technique called "Virtual Cinematography." This innovation allowed animators to create a virtual 360-degree set, where they could place hand-drawn characters, creating depth and precise positioning in each scene. They could also move the camera freely, just like on a real movie set.

This tech was first used in "Tarzan" for about 10% of the film (remember the tree surfing?). "Treasure Planet" followed the "70/30 rule": 70% traditional 2D animation and 30% CGI.

Legendary 🤩

4. Blending Past and Future

To create a 19th-century look, the animators used illustrations from the original "Treasure Island" as inspiration, especially N.C. Wyeth's. These images helped set the film's unique atmosphere.

Unused concept art from "Tarzan" also helped shape "Treasure Planet"'s visuals. Many of the same artists worked on both films, and their jungle designs became the basis for the flora on Captain Flint's planet.

The filmmakers used the "70/30 rule" for the film's themes: 70% past, 30% future. This meant the characters didn't have modern inventions like TV, microwaves, or cell phones, but their ships had advanced computers and navigation systems.

Treasure Planet itself was a complex mechanism opened by a spherical keycard that led to other galaxies.

Character Changes:

◇ **Jim Hawkins:** In the book, he's a smart, capable 15-year-old. In the movie, he's a rebellious teen with a run-in with the law, making him more relatable to modern audiences.

◇ **Dr. Doppler:** He combines Dr. Livesey and Squire Trelawney from the book, making him a serious scientist who's also a bit of a bumbling fool.

◇ **Cyborg Silver:** In the book, he's Long John Silver. In the movie, he develops a fatherly bond with Jim, which is a significant change. Directors wanted a "father-son" dynamic, connecting Jim to Silver emotionally, not just professionally.

◇ **John Silver's parrot** is replaced by Morph, a shapeshifting alien.

5. The Birth of a Rebellious Hero

Creating Jim Hawkins was a challenge for the animators. The directors envisioned him as a troubled teen at a crossroads with an uncertain future. He could go down a dark path, but he also had the potential to become a good person. His rebellious nature stemmed from losing his father.

For inspiration, the animators looked to James Dean, a 1950s American actor known for playing complex, rebellious character.

Dean's inner turmoil, hesitant speech, and sensitivity were all incorporated into Jim Hawkins' animated portrayal. Sixteen animators worked to capture these traits in the film.

Character Study:

- ◇ To understand 15-year-old Jim's psychology, the directors studied books on child development and teenage psychology and watched movies about teenage rebels.

- ◇ Actor Joseph Gordon-Levitt, who voiced Jim, played a crucial role in shaping his character. If he felt a line didn't sound like a teenager, he would suggest a better one, making Jim more believable and natural.

Curious: According to his mother, he built his first solar surfer at age 8.

> **Funny Fact:** Imagine those animators suddenly saying stuff like, "Dude, that sketch is rad!" after watching all those teen flicks. 😂

"You shine like the sun. You're special, Jim. You'll reach the stars." – John Silver

6. A Solar Surfer's Journey

At the beginning of the film, Jim uses his homemade solar surfer to seek thrills, landing him in trouble with the police.

He's portrayed as a typical rebellious teenager seeking attention and challenge.

However, by the end of the film, we see Jim use his solar surfing skills to save himself and his friends on Treasure Planet. This scene marks his transformation from a reckless teen to a responsible young man, willing to risk himself for others. He shifts from seeking personal adventure to finding meaning and purpose. Talk about a 180!

In the ending, the same police officers escort Jim back to the rebuilt Benbow Inn. This time, they meet him as a hero, not a troubled young man. This moment emphasizes Jim's full character arc, confirming his transformation into a mature and responsible hero.

Curious: Jim's dark hair gradually lightens as the story progresses, reflecting his transition from "bad boy" to "hero."

7. Hidden Clues in the Heroes' Rooms

The main characters' rooms often contain hidden clues about their personalities, the plot, or unusual secrets. For example, Jim Hawkins' shelf features a ship and a robot (which appear later in the story), and also Stitch from the movie "Lilo & Stitch," which was released a few months earlier.

Rare

8. Mechanical Mastery: The Lifelike Cyborg Silver

Eric Daniels, a computer animation pioneer and co-creator of "virtual cinematography," played a crucial role in bringing John Silver to life in Treasure Planet. He meticulously animated Silver's mechanical arm, right eye, and leg, working closely with Glen Keane, who animated the character's hand-drawn parts.

Daniels wanted Silver's mechanical limbs to look like old-fashioned, functional ironwork rather than shiny new gadgets. He studied 19th-century heavy machinery for inspiration.

Interestingly, Silver embodies the "70/30" principle used in Treasure Planet. His artificial eye has a laser beam and other technological advancements, reminiscent of James Cameron's Terminator. On the other hand, his built-in handgun is a simple musket, typical of 300-year-old weaponry.

Silver's mechanical arm contains various tools, including an egg holder inspired by a cherry and olive holder. It also has cutters, carving knives, and even a blowtorch. Keane and Daniels worked hard to integrate these elements into one arm, like a Swiss Army knife, allowing Silver to use them skillfully. They also avoided turning the character into a caricature like Inspector Gadget with absurd gadgets. Silver's arm had to be realistic and believable, not just a cartoonish prop.

Curious: Animator Glen Keane kept Silver's fatherly relationship with Jim Hawkins in mind while designing the cyborg. He drew inspiration from his own personal experiences and memories. In particular, Glen often thought of his own son to better understand the character and reflect his warmth and protectiveness.

9. Silver's Sneer and Speech

Glen Keane, the animator behind Silver, got inspiration from all sorts of places. He took a page out of Wallace Beery's book (the actor who played a pirate in Treasure Island) and gave Silver Beery's signature "talking out of the side of his mouth" style.

Another key part of Silver's look was his teeth. They were inspired by Brian Murray, the actor who voiced Silver. Murray is Irish and has a habit of showing his upper teeth when he talks. Keane found this interesting and after meeting with Murray, he drew a bunch of caricatures of him and put them up by his desk. So, when Silver talks in the movie, you can see his teeth, too. But Keane added a little gap between Silver's teeth to keep them from looking too perfect, making the character more unique and realistic.

Curious: To create the scene where Jim and Silver meet in the ship's galley and Silver shows off his cooking skills, the animators visited a Benihana restaurant kitchen and studied how to chop shrimp.

* Rare *

10. B.E.N.: Creating a Unique Digital Character

B.E.N. is special because he's the only character in the movie that was completely computer-animated. Oskar Urretabizkaia, who had previously worked on Hydra in Hercules, was the lead animator for B.E.N. It took him two years to bring the energetic robot to life.

Interestingly, B.E.N. was originally supposed to be a quiet, nervous loner. He was supposed to be very suspicious of people after meeting them. But after actor Martin Short signed on to voice the robot, B.E.N.'s character changed a lot. He became this wild, spazztastic character with a rapid-fire speaking style and a voice that would suddenly go high-pitched.

B.E.N.'s role in the story was also supposed to be smaller. He was just supposed to show the heroes the way to the planet's core. But thanks to Martin Short's charisma, the animators pushed to give the character more screen time. As John Musker said, "Short immediately latched onto two key aspects of B.E.N. - his touchiness and his talkativeness. That helped us shape the character. He talks too much and touches too much, like a long-lost relative who's trying to make up for lost time. He's the opposite of Jim Hawkins, who's withdrawn and doesn't like to be touched." So, thanks to Short's talent, we got a lot more B.E.N. in the movie.

Curious: When B.E.N. is seen without his memory chip, his eyes are green. When he regains his memory at the climax of the movie and reboots, his eyes turn blue and stay that way for the rest of the movie.

11. The Spaceship's Secret Name

The spaceship R.L.S. Legacy plays a crucial role in the movie. This name is only mentioned once by Dr. Doppler when he and Jim arrive at the port. However, it has a deeper meaning: R.L.S. are the initials of the famous author of "Treasure Island," Robert Louis Stevenson. In some translated versions, the ship is called "Stevenson's Legacy," which accurately reflects this fact.

12. Breaking the Disney Villain Mold

Scroop's fate stands out from the traditional Disney villain death scenarios. Usually, Disney animated movies feature villains falling to their deaths, like Gaston in "Beauty and the Beast" or the Evil Queen in "Snow White." However, in Treasure Planet, Scroop doesn't fall down but rather rises up to his demise, making him unique among Disney villains.

> **Funny Fact:** Maybe Scroop thought falling was too cliché for a villain of his caliber. "Why not have a farewell flight? To the black hole, please!"

★ Rare ★

13. Hidden Humor in Dr. Doppler's Menu

Dr. Doppler, the dog-like alien character, mentions eating "Alponian chowder" in one scene. This name is a pun, referencing the well-known American dog food brand Alpo.

This is an example of the subtle humor Disney often uses in its movies, including puns and references.

> **Funny Fact:** When Doppler ordered "Alponian chowder,",he probably added: "And please, hold the dog food. I'm feeling particularly picky today!"

14. Treasure Planet: One of Disney's Most Underrated?

The film Treasure Planet flopped at the box office, not even recouping its production costs. This is doubly surprising because Treasure Planet has a fairly high rating with both audiences and critics.

Curious: The cartoon is included in the lists: Most Expensive Movies and Top 100 Animated Films of All Time.

> **Funny Fact:** A forgotten treasure that wasn't found right away, but worth searching for! I recommend you boldly go on a space adventure - you might find something that the movie theaters missed!

The Map to Treasure Planet ◇ 81

BROTHER BEAR

1. Alaskan Adventure

In 2000, the animation team ventured into the wild lands of Alaska to study Kodiak bears and immerse themselves in Native American culture.

This real-life experience helped them create a truly authentic and captivating animation for "Brother Bear."

Curious: The film was initially called "Bears."

2. Hidden Geography

Eagle-eyed viewers might notice that some character names are actual locations in Alaska and Canada!

For example, Sitka and Kenai are Alaskan cities, and Tanana is a river tributary in the Yukon.

These geographical references add a layer of depth and realism to the story.

* Rare *

3. Changing Paws

Kenai's companion was initially envisioned as Grizz, a massive adult bear resembling the wise bear, Tug.

However, Grizz failed to evoke the desired emotional connection with the audience.

As a result, he was replaced by the adorable bear cub, Koda, who brought a heartwarming emotional element to the story.

Curious: Another reason for Koda's younger age was to portray Kenai as a responsible older brother figure rather than a rebellious younger one.

Brother Bear ◇ 83

Interestingly, Koda's name means "tail" in the Alutiiq language.

4. Totem Symbolism in "Brother Bear"

The animated film "Brother Bear" features three significant totems, each representing unique qualities and characteristics:

4.1 The Falcon

Symbolizes: Adventure

Person with this totem:

- ◇ Highly active
- ◇ Vibrant individual
- ◇ Doesn't risk for the sake of discovery
- ◇ Strong in spirit and body

Destiny: Success and extraordinary adventures

4.2 The Otter

Symbolizes: Playfulness, carefree nature, discernment, courage

Person with this totem:

- ◇ Most courageous and creative
- ◇ Finds joy in the thought of traveling

4.3 The Wolf

Symbolizes: Empathy, compassion, understanding, honesty

Person with this totem:

- ⋄ Will find many friends in life
- ⋄ Shows compassion and support
- ⋄ Friends reciprocate

Destiny: Worthy of pride

These totems play a crucial role in guiding and shaping the characters' journeys.

5. From Human Eyes to Bear Vision

One of the unique aspects of the film is the use of aspect ratio as a storytelling device. Before Kenai's transformation into a bear, the film is presented in a 1.75:1 aspect ratio. However, shortly after the transformation, the format changes to 2.35:1. Along with this change, the style and color palette shift slightly - after the transformation, the world appears before Kenai's (and the viewer's) eyes in brighter, more ethereal tones. These techniques are used to illustrate the differences in how humans and bears perceive reality.

Curious: Kenai is the third Disney protagonist of Native American descent (Inuit, in Kenai's case), with Pocahontas being the first and Kuzco the second.

Kenai's age is never explicitly stated in the films, although he is most likely around 16 years old, as 12-16 is considered the age of maturity in First Nations tribes.

6. When Words are Lost

In "Brother Bear," Denahi experiences an intriguing transformation. After Kenai becomes a bear, Denahi largely falls silent, expressing himself through growls and yells, especially during his conflicts with Kenai. He remains speechless until pivotal moments – shouting "No!" when a bridge collapses, warming himself by a fire, and ultimately when Kenai transforms back into a human.

This change in Denahi is probably because, as the wise Tanana says, bears and humans can't talk to each other. So, when Kenai tries to talk to Denahi as a bear, Denahi only hears bear growls, not his brother's words.

ANIMATING BOLT

1. Finding Inspiration for Bolt

To create a believable and captivating world for the animated film "Bolt," Disney's animation team went on an extensive research trip across the United States. Their mission was to sketch real houses, streets, and landscapes that would form the foundation of the film's backgrounds and animation.

Their extensive journey led them to these diverse landscapes:

- ◊ **Los Angeles and New York City:** The energy and scale of these metropolises inspired the film's vibrant cityscapes.

- ◊ **The Nevada Desert:** The desert's vastness provided the perfect setting for thrilling chase scenes.

- ◊ **A Trailer Park in Ohio:** The animators captured the essence of typical American RVs found in the film.

- ◊ **The Port of San Francisco:** This bustling port with its ships and docks served as inspiration for the shipboard scene.

- ◊ **Las Vegas Casinos:** The dazzling lights and extravagance of this gambling city set the stage for the final showdown.

Curious: Bolt's appearance was a blend of different dog breeds, with the White Swiss Shepherd serving as the primary inspiration. His signature pointed ears and fluffy tail were drawn directly from this breed.

To accurately capture Bolt's movements, animators used special suits fitted with sensors to record the natural movements of real dogs and translate them into the animation.

2. From Fiction to Reality

When Bolt escapes from the studio, he wears a dog collar and has a lightning bolt drawn on his fur. These two symbols represent his loyalty to Penny and his superhero illusion. Later, when he returns to Penny after his adventure, the collar remains, but the lightning bolt sign is smudged, symbolizing his realization and departure from the superhero role while maintaining his connection with Penny.

Curious: John Travolta lends his voice to Bolt, bringing a unique character to the lovable and determined dog. Miley Cyrus voices Penny, Bolt's owner and best friend. The end credits of the film feature the song "I Thought I Lost You," performed by John Travolta and Miley Cyrus, further contributing to the film's memorable soundtrack.

Rare

3. Creating Rhino 🐹

Rhino, the hamster, proved to be one of the most challenging characters to bring to life in "Bolt."

To ensure his movements were as realistic as possible, the studio brought in a real hamster. The team filmed the hamster from below as it moved across a transparent surface, meticulously studying its unique movement patterns. Rhino's overall appearance was inspired by the chinchilla.

THE PRINCESS AND THE FROG

1. Fairy Tale Epidemic 😲 🐸

Believe it or not, when "The Princess and the Frog" hit theaters, around 50 kids ended up hospitalized with salmonella! Turns out, they all went searching for enchanted princes to kiss and break the spell.

> **Funny Fact:** This movie didn't just provide a fairytale – it ended up as an unplanned biology lesson for these young explorers. Lesson learned: Maybe next time, search for princes in a cleaner environment...like a library! 😊

2. Crafting Tiana

Anika Noni Rose, who voiced Princess Tiana in "The Princess and the Frog," requested that the character be left-handed, like herself.

Curious: Tiana's adorable dimples were also inspired by the actress herself.

3. The Green Card Mystery: A Look Through Symbols

If the prince were good at spotting hidden clues, he would've seen his fate coming a mile away! The sorcerer hints: "Jump from place to place. But for freedom, you need green" and "Now try to guess the color of destiny," showing a map covered in green. The greedy prince sees money in the color green, completely missing the hint he'll be hopping around as a frog! And if we take a closer look, even tiny frogs are hidden within the green markings on the map!

Legendary 😃

4. From Human to Crocodile

Get this: in an early version of "The Princess and the Frog," Louis wasn't always an alligator! He started out as a human with dreams of playing an instrument. He seeks help from Dr. Facilier, who turns him into a musical genius – with the unfortunate side effect of changing him into a crocodile. Talk about a plot twist! The creators ultimately decided this was a tad too confusing for the story, so they went in a different direction.

Curious: If Louis the trumpet-playing alligator feels familiar, it's because he was featured in an episode of the classic 90s cartoon "Chip 'n Dale Rescue Rangers"!

THE MAKING OF TANGLED

1. Golden Hair

It's wild to think that Disney's "Tangled" cost more to make than the groundbreaking "Avatar"! With a budget of $260 million, "Tangled" became the most expensive animated film ever, stealing that title from "Avatar" ($237 million). Did you know it was also Disney's 50th animated film? It marked a serious milestone for the company!

> **Funny Fact:** Rapunzel's hair is over 70 feet long! Can you imagine how long it would take her to dry it after a shower?

2. Animating Rapunzel's Luscious Locks

Rapunzel's golden mane is about 70 feet long and has over 100,000 individual strands of hair! It took some serious computer magic to make it move realistically on screen. Animators used a special program called Dynamic Wires to bring her hair to life. It was the most detailed hair animation done in any movie up to that point.

Did you know the average person's hair is only about 12 inches long? Put all the strands together, and they stretch about 26 miles. Rapunzel's hair would go on for over 1,820 miles!

Curious: One of the animators who worked on the hair simulation program, Kelly Ward, even wrote a dissertation on computer animation of hair. She is a leading expert in this field and continues to work on hair animation in the film industry.

Another interesting fact is that 10 women from the creative team decided to grow their hair out during the production of the film. When they were finished, they cut it off and donated it to an organization that makes wigs for people who have lost their hair due to illness.

* Rare *

3. Balancing Weight and Movement in Animation

The iconic 70-feet long hair of Rapunzel from Disney's "Tangled" was a significant challenge for animators. Kelly Ward, a senior software engineer at Walt Disney Animation Studios, calculated that in reality, such hair would weigh between 60 to 80 pounds. However, for the movie, animators needed to balance this realism with the need for Rapunzel's hair to move fluidly and interact naturally with her surroundings. To achieve this, they cleverly manipulated the physics in the animation to make the hair appear both weighty and manageable for the character's movements. This creative approach was part of the innovative techniques used to bring Rapunzel's character to life.

4. The Hidden Message of Rapunzel's Barefoot Journey

Rapunzel's constant barefoot appearance carries symbolic meaning. It represents her naivety and innocence, having been sheltered in the tower her entire life. Plus, it hints at Mother Gothel's control — like she's saying that Rapunzel doesn't even need shoes because she shouldn't try to leave. This adds another layer to Rapunzel's story and her struggle to break free.

5. Secret Symbols in the Tower

The animators paid homage to previous Disney movies in a clever way! During her long time in the tower, Rapunzel decorated it with drawings. The ones on the staircase pillars are especially interesting, as they reference past Disney princesses: an apple for Snow White, a slipper for Cinderella, a rose for Belle, and a seashell for Ariel.

> **Funny Fact:** Who says being locked in a tower is boring? I have my own art gallery!

6. Guided by Light

Rapunzel always dreamed of finding out about the floating lanterns that appeared in the sky on her birthday every year. At first, she even thought they were stars. It was her desire to learn about the lanterns that became her main motivation to escape the tower.

During the lantern festival, Rapunzel managed to catch the one launched by her parents. When she sails on the boat with Flynn, you can see a lantern with a sun symbol flying towards her - it's the royal emblem, and there are no others like it. So, she really did catch her parents' lantern!

Curious Fact: The animators initially wanted to use fireworks, but the production designer came up with the idea of using lanterns. Way more magical! 🏮 ✨

In the climax of the film, you can see a whopping 46,000 lanterns! It's hard to imagine, but each light consists of 10,000 tiny drawn light beams!

7. The Squirrel that Became a Chameleon

In the early stages of development, Rapunzel's charming companion was actually supposed to be a squirrel. Pascal was envisioned as a fluffy, long-tailed cutie, but later, he was based on a real chameleon owned by one of the studio employees! After it was decided that Pascal should be a reptile, Disney considered making him purple. But, in the end, the green chameleon was the best fit, also matching Rapunzel's dress.

8. Maximus Uses a Roman Sword ⚔

In the battle with Flynn, Maximus, one of the film's most memorable characters, wields a Roman sword - this is clear from its shape. This Easter egg references his name, which means "greatest," reminding us of that epic Roman general Maximus from "Gladiator"!

9. Maximus and Pascal Were Voiced by the Same Person

Frank Welker, a legendary voice actor with over 800 credits to his name, actually voiced both Maximus and Pascal!

Welker is known for his animal and creature voices: he voiced 16 characters in Futurama, and he's also the voice of Fred Jones and Scooby-Doo! He's also worked on other Disney movies like Aladdin, The Little Mermaid, Pocahontas, and many more.

10. Who Was the Inspiration for Flynn Rider?

Flynn Rider was originally supposed to be a British farmer, but his character evolved into the charming thief we know and love. He was inspired by characters like Han Solo and Indiana Jones.

11. One Detail Shows That Mother Gothel Doesn't Really Love Rapunzel

Some fans think Mother Gothel loved Rapunzel, even in her own twisted way. But here's the truth: when Gothel says "I love you most," she kisses Rapunzel's HAIR, not her forehead. All she cares about is staying young and pretty thanks to that magic hair!

* Rare *

12. Mother Gothel's Age Mystery

We can get a clue about Mother Gothel's age from the character's clothing. Their styles are very different. Gothel's dress resembles Renaissance clothing, which began in the 1300s. The action of the cartoon takes place in the late 1700s. This means that Mother Gothel is at least 400 years old. So, her attempts to regain her youth seem quite justified.

Funny Fact: Mother Gothel's so old, her first pet was probably a dinosaur, not Pascal!

13. The Largest Animated Gathering

The film features five main characters, 21 thugs, and 38 townspeople. For the climactic lantern scene, the special effects artists were tasked with bringing 3,000 townspeople to the screen. At the time, it was the largest crowd scene in Disney computer animation history.

14. From Normandy to Fantasy

The kingdom of Corona was inspired by one of the most visited places in France - Mont Saint-Michel on the coast of

Normandy, which receives almost 2.5 million visitors each year.

Curious: The island is still home to 44 people, including monks and nuns who live in the abbey. Moreover, the monastery was the inspiration for the city of Minas Tirith, a location in The Lord of the Rings.

15. Yosemite's Influence on 'Tangled'

The waterfall and rushing river near Rapunzel's tower were inspired by the rivers and waterfalls in Yosemite National Park in California. Over 150 nature videos were shot from there, which the artists used to choose the best locations and angles.

Curious: Did you know that it takes over 10 million individual droplets to draw a waterfall?

BRAVE

1. Following Merida's Footsteps

To create a realistic world for "Brave," the Disney-Pixar crew traveled to Scotland. These trips were a true source of inspiration for artists, animators, and screenwriters.

Edinburgh and the Royal Mile: During their visits to Scotland, the filmmakers visited Edinburgh, the country's capital. They wandered through the narrow streets of the Old Town, visited authentic shops, and walked along the famous Royal Mile, where medieval city life is in full swing.

A Taste of Scotland: Traditional Scottish food was also on the menu. The crew tried haggis - a national dish of sheep's offal - as well as other Scottish treats.

National Museum of Scotland: To immerse themselves in the country's history and culture, the animators visited the National Museum of Scotland. In its collection, they saw examples of ancient weapons, fabrics, jewelry, and other everyday objects that helped them recreate the atmosphere of medieval Scotland in the cartoon.

Thanks to these trips, "Brave" turned out to be not just a beautiful and funny story but also a story about life in Scotland in the past.

Curious: Disney animators used photographs taken in Scotland to create realistic landscapes. The cartoon features traditional Scottish melodies.

2. Why the First Curly-Haired Princess Appeared So Late

Initially, the creators of "The Little Mermaid" wanted to give Ariel beautiful curly hair, but alas, the computer graphics of 1989 did not allow it. Therefore, the first curly-haired Disney princess was Merida from "Brave" - and it only happened in 2012. Over the course of 3 years, a special simulator was created that predicted the behavior of 1,500 curls. Just imagine: the scene where Merida takes off her hood and her curls fly apart took two months to create.

Curious: One of the animators suggested that Merida's unruly curls curl on the same principle as a spiral telephone cord. This is the idea that formed the basis of the main character's hairstyle! By the way, Merida's hair is made up of 1,500 individual strands.

If Merida straightened her curls, her hair would be over a meter long.

> **Funny Fact:** Of course, it can't be compared to Rapunzel's curls, but what curls!

3. We don't know how Merida sings

In Disney-Pixar's "Brave," Princess Merida stands out not just for her fiery red hair and unmatched archery skills but also for her distinct lack of a singing performance, a common trait among her fellow Disney princesses. This distinction might suggest that the spirited Merida, ever the activist, simply does not find the time to sing amidst her adventures.

Unlike their counterpart princesses, who often explore themes of love and romance through their songs, Merida's story is driven by her quest for independence and self-discovery. Her narrative breaks the mold by focusing on personal strength and the bond between mother and daughter, without relying on musical numbers to express her inner thoughts and feelings.

This creative choice underscores Merida's unique position in the Disney Princess lineup as a symbol of bravery, freedom, further highlighting her role as a modern heroine who challenges traditional expectations.

ABOUT FROZEN

1. Walt Disney Started Working on Frozen in the 1940s

Did you know that the idea for "Frozen" may have come from Walt Disney himself, all the way back in the 1940s? That's right, Walt was ahead of his time!

In 1943, Disney began adapting Hans Christian Andersen's fairy tale "The Snow Queen" into an animated feature film. However, the project was shelved for decades, and Walt never got to see it become a Disney movie.

So why did the studio heads decide to revisit "Frozen" after so many years? It all had to do with the success of "Tangled."

2. The Norwegian Influence

The movie is filled with references to Norway, from the name of Anna's horse, "Kjekk" (which means "Handsome" in Norwegian) to the landscapes of Arendelle, which were inspired by the Norwegian countryside. The crew even visited Norway to capture the beauty of its lakes and fjords.

There are also elements of Norwegian culture in the film, including Vikings and Scandinavian runes. A Scandinavian mythology expert, Jackson Crawford, helped the animators with the correct depiction of the runes.

3. Frozen's Icy Inspiration

For the creation of Elsa's ice palace, the animation team undertook an inspiring journey to Quebec, Canada. They visited the Hotel de Glace, a unique ice hotel, which significantly influenced the design and ambiance of Elsa's palace.

The hotel then capitalized on this connection by creating a

special "Frozen" themed room with a Disney-inspired bed fit for a princess, further intertwining the realms of animation and reality.

4. The Making the Most Time-Consuming Shot

The creation of the longest shot took an astounding 132 hours. That's the scene where Elsa steps onto the balcony of her newly formed ice palace, surveying the landscape around her. The complexity of this scene stemmed from various elements: Elsa's hair (all 400,000 strands), her shimmering dress, the sparkling ice, and the intricate way light interacts with each element. Additionally, Dr. Kenneth Libbrecht, a renowned snow expert, was consulted to ensure the authenticity of the snow scenes.

Curious: When Hans talks to Elsa in prison, you can see his breath. But when Elsa speaks, there is no steam coming from her mouth because she has ice powers.

5. Frozen Shatters Disney's Glass Ceiling

In 2013, Disney made history with "Frozen." It was the first time a full-length animated feature was co-directed by a woman, Jennifer Lee. That's a big deal, considering Disney has been around since the early 1930s!

Not only that, but Lee became the first female director to have a film gross over $1 billion at the box office. Lee is breaking barriers all over the film industry!

Legendary 😍

6. Elsa Was Almost the Movie's Villain

In the early stages of development, Elsa and Anna weren't sisters, and Elsa was an evil sorceress (like her "Snow Queen" inspiration). Anna would have gone to her to ask her to freeze her broken heart.

Elsa was originally going to have blue skin and a weasel fur coat.

The script changed after the movie's signature song, "Let It Go," was written. The song gave Elsa a new purpose and transformed her from a villain into a complex young woman. "Let It Go" was translated into 41 languages.

Curious: When original songstress Idina Menzel recorded "Let It Go," animators were in the studio capturing her every move. They used this footage to make Elsa's performance as authentic as possible. It took 600 people two and a half years to fully animate the characters.

7. Only Two Disney Princesses Have Magic Powers ✨

While magic is often a part of Disney movie plots, it's rare for the princesses themselves to have magical abilities. There are only two exceptions: Rapunzel with her healing, glowing hair, and Elsa with her icy powers. ❄

For fans of Rapunzel and Elsa's magical abilities, here's a gateway to another enchanting world of magic: "Harry Potter Spellbook: The Unofficial Illustrated Guide to Wizard Training." This book is a collection of spells and instructions for using magic from the world of Harry Potter. Search for it on Amazon to begin your journey into a new magical world. Your knowledge of spells will be a bridge between the world of Disney and the rich legacy of Harry Potter magic.

8. Elsa's Ice Palace Changes Color with Her Mood 🌈 🏰

When she's happy, the castle is blue. When she's scared, it turns red. When she's angry, it's yellow. And when she's sad, it's purple.

Curious: Elsa loves chocolate.

> **Funny Fact:** Imagine how fun it would be to hang out at Elsa's place with her ever-changing mood castle! You wouldn't even need a disco ball!

9. The Symbolism of Hair: Anna and Elsa's Journey to Unity

Anna's white hair streak is a subtle detail that highlights the sisters' separation. It appeared when Elsa accidentally injured Anna with her magic as a child, leading to their estrangement. But the streak disappears in the film's finale, symbolizing the sisters overcoming their challenges and getting closer again.

10. Elsa's Platinum Blonde

Many people might think Elsa has gray or white hair, but it actually has a subtle blonde tone. Elsa's hair is platinum blonde, the lightest shade of blonde. Her magical gift is what makes her hair so light. In fact, her hair would be the same color as Anna's if not for her magic.

Curious: "Frozen" is the first Disney animated film with two main female characters. Previously, Disney princess stories focused on the romance between a beautiful princess and a prince. But "Frozen" is different - it centers on the relationship between two sisters. Anna's romantic storyline is secondary; she meets Hans and Kristoff by chance while pursuing her own goals. Elsa doesn't have a romantic storyline at all; her focus is on self-realization and understanding herself, her magical gift, and her purpose in life.

11. Pioneering Characters

Elsa holds the distinction of being the first Disney film heroine whose coronation is shown to the audience. Previously, only Princess Kidagakash from "Atlantis: The Lost Empire" became a queen, but her ascension to the throne wasn't depicted on screen. Additionally, Anna from "Frozen" also had a unique debut. She is the first positive character to sing a duet with a villain (Prince Hans), even though she was unaware of his true nature at the time.

12. Elsa: Disney's Oldest Princess at 24

Elsa holds the title of the oldest Disney princess (or queen?) as she turns 24 in the sequel. This age sets her apart from the typical age range of Disney princesses, with the youngest being Snow White at just 14. In "Frozen 2," Anna is 21, making them the oldest sibling pair in Disney films. Most princesses are around 16, including Merida, Ariel, Aurora, Moana, and Mulan. Jasmine is 15, Pocahontas and Rapunzel are 18, while Tiana and Cinderella are 19, and Belle is 17. Now you know!

* Rare *

13. Kristoff's Connection with Norway's Sámi People

Kristoff's character in Disney's "Frozen" was significantly influenced by the Sámi people of Northern Norway. Kristoff is depicted as an ice harvester, a once-real profession in Norway. Ice harvesting was a major industry, supplying ice for both domestic and commercial use in Scandinavia and the USA. The Sámi people, known primarily for reindeer herding, also engaged in this craft. This cultural reference is why Kristoff is accompanied by his loyal reindeer, Sven, in the film.

14. Disney's Whimsical Disclaimer on Kristoff's Quirky Thoughts

The end credits include a humorous disclaimer stating that the opinions expressed by Kristoff about men eating their own boogers are not necessarily those of the Walt Disney Company. This tongue-in-cheek note refers to a line Kristoff says during a conversation with Anna in the film.

> **Funny Fact:** If you ever dine in Arendelle, you might want to skip Kristoff's special. 😄

15. Sven - Definitely One of the Cutest Characters in the Movie

The character of Sven, Kristoff's loyal reindeer companion, was a challenge for the animators to bring to life. Initially, they brought in a real reindeer to study its movements and behavior, but the animal was uncooperative, refusing to move. This led to a creative solution: the animators decided to observe the dog of executive producer John Lasseter. They found inspiration in the dog's movements, which helped them capture Sven's unique and endearing character traits, blending reindeer and canine mannerisms to create Sven's memorable and lovable personality.

Curious: Sven wasn't always going to be called Sven. His original name was Thor!

16. Olaf's Improv: The Spontaneous Snowman ☃

Olaf, the lovable snowman, became a fan favorite for his humorous personality and his naive understanding of snowmen's fate in summer. What makes Olaf's character even more special is that actor Josh Gad, who voiced Olaf, largely improvised his lines. Much like Robin Williams' iconic performance in "Aladdin," Gad's spontaneous humor during the recording sessions brought a unique and comical element to Olaf's character. This approach was initially to entertain the producers, but many of these improvised lines were so fitting and humorous they were included in the final version of the film.

17. Olaf Embodies Elsa and Anna's Happiness

Olaf's very existence shows how much Elsa's isolation from Anna affected her. The first voluntary act Elsa does with her powers is to build a snowman, something Anna had been asking her to do for years. She sings "Let It Go" while creating him, showing how much she longed to play with her sister. It's possible that the strength of that desire brought Olaf to life.

Curious: The destruction of the original Olaf marked the end of Elsa and Anna's carefree childhood friendship. Also, like Anna and Elsa's friendship, the original Olaf was destroyed because Elsa's powers spiraled out of control due to her inner turmoil.

18. The Distinctive Dress of Prince Hans

Prince Hans doesn't come from Arendelle, so his outfits were designed to be different. They used graphic elements and some decorative Norwegian art styles to show this.

Curious: Hans, Kristoff, Anna, and Sven together sound like Hans Christian Andersen, who wrote the story "The Snow Queen," on which the movie is based.

19. The Sinister Reflection

Parts of Hans were inspired by the evil mirror in the original

Snow Queen story. It's said that anyone who looked in the mirror would see their darkest side revealed. If a piece of it got into someone's body, their heart would freeze cold.

Jennifer Lee (the director) confirmed that Hans was partly based on that mirror idea. She says he's like a mirror – charming on the outside, but basically "empty or sociopathic" inside.

Curious: Hans is like a dark version of Anna. Both were isolated from siblings and felt alone. But while Anna stayed loving and optimistic, Hans got bitter and ice-cold.

* Rare *

20. A Villain in Disguise

Hans represents a quite unique type of Disney villain. Unlike traditional antagonists, whose malevolent nature is apparent from the beginning, Hans initially appears benevolent and trustworthy. This distinguishes him from characters such as Scar from "The Lion King," whose evil intentions become quickly evident to the viewer, despite the trust other main characters may have in them. Hans, however, successfully conceals his true goals, creating an illusion of sincere interest in Anna and her well-being. His betrayal is only revealed closer to the film's climax, becoming a real surprise for both the characters and the audience. This unexpected twist makes Hans one of the most memorable Disney villains, as he breaks the conventional mold of presenting antagonists in fairy tales.

Curious: There are actually subtle hints throughout the movie that foreshadow Hans' villainy before his big reveal:

> ◇ **Dreaming of the Crown.** When Hans falls into the water and lifts the boat, a dreamy expression crosses his face. It's possible he's fantasizing about the crown at this moment.

About Frozen ◇ 111

⋄ **Selfish Motives.** Anna wants to find Elsa, but Hans tries to dissuade her, citing the potential danger. However, his real reason is the fear of losing his chance to become king since he hasn't married her yet.

⋄ **Thirst for Power.** When Anna appoints Hans as regent, his objections immediately disappear. His eyes light up with excitement, as he sees this as a chance to get the power he desires.

21. Elsa and Anna as Baby Name Inspiration

After the movie came out, the names Elsa and Anna became super popular for newborn girls. Elsa, previously not a very common name, entered the top 100 most popular names for the first time in 2013. Anna, already a well-known and widely used name, also became even more popular. This rise in popularity shows how much the movie influenced cultural trends.

22. Real-Life Rescue Tune

In Boston, two firefighters calmed down a little girl stuck in an elevator with the song "Let It Go"! Kristen Kerr, her baby son, and her daughter Kaelin were trapped on the second floor. Firefighters John Keefe and Scott Moyett talked with the family over the intercom and figured out Kaelin was freaked out. So, they started singing the mega-hit from the movie. It helped relax the girl, and the firefighters were able to safely evacuate them via the emergency stairs.

BIG HERO 6

1. A Blend of Two Worlds

In the exciting world of "Big Hero 6," there's a city called San Fransokyo. Guess what? It's a mix of two amazing cities - San Francisco and Tokyo! Imagine having the fun and busy streets of Tokyo mixed with the cool, hilly vibes of San Francisco. It wasn't easy to create this fantastic city in the movie. A talented artist named Lorelay Bove helped bring San Fransokyo to life. She had a super creative idea to put Victorian houses, like the ones in San Francisco, right on the streets of Tokyo.

Curious: The creative team took a research trip to Japan, where they were amazed by the thoughtfulness of design, detail, and finish in everything from trash cans to vending machines to sidewalk tiles. These observations were reflected in the look of San Fransokyo.

2. A Growing Team

The animated film was created by a team of over 100 people - 103 to be exact. For comparison, the 2013 animated hit "Frozen" had a team of 88 people.

Curious: The characters have interesting and unusual modern hobbies to go with their superhero lives! For example, Honey Lemon collects bright cell phone cases, and Fred collects vintage comics and loves yoga.

3. An Army of Characters

To create the crowd scenes, the directors used a special computer program called Denizen, developed by Walt Disney Animation Studios animators. They managed to create 670 unique characters for the crowd scenes:

Each character had over 32 variations of clothing, hairstyles, and skin tones. This allowed the creators to populate San Fransokyo with 686,080 unique characters.

Access to the Denizen program was open to all Walt Disney Animation Studios employees, so everyone could create their own prototype in the system. As a result, over 200 members of the animation team can find themselves in one of the inhabitants of densely populated San Fransokyo.

4. From Comic to Screen

"Big Hero 6" isn't exactly like the 1998 Marvel comic it's based on. They changed a lot of stuff – the characters' backgrounds, how they look, and even parts of the storyline. Disney chose this comic because it wasn't super popular. That way, fans would go see the movie without comparing it to a beloved comic series.

5. Rocket Cat That Never Was

Legendary 🤩

Like any other big-budget animated film, "Big Hero 6" went through many different versions of the story. According to Paul Briggs, the head of story, there were about 40 variations of the opening scene alone!

One of the early ideas involved Hiro creating Rocket Cat, which would have been his pet cat Mochi with rocket boosters so he could zoom through the air. However, Mochi didn't make it into the final version of the movie, and many animators were sad to see him go. They even imagined all the hilarious memes that could have been created with this character!

Interestingly, Japanese promoters who saw test footage of Rocket Cat loved him so much that they included him in the promotional campaign. It was only shortly before the premiere that they were told Mochi wouldn't be in the movie.

Curious: Fans of Mochi decided to keep his memory alive by creating a Tumblr blog in his honor. The blog features various fan art and opinions about why this cute character should have been in the movie.

> **Funny Fact:** Mochi, eyeing those rocket boosters: "My tail definitely doesn't approve of this idea!" 🐱

6. Inspired by Koalas and Penguins 🐨 🐧

In Japanese pop culture, robots are often seen as a key to an optimistic future, so the animators wanted to give Baymax a friendly and approachable appearance. His facial expressions, gestures, and overall look were inspired by koalas and penguins, animals that people find cute and endearing.

Rare

7. Baymax's Movement Magic

The animation team coined the term "unimation" when it came to animating Baymax due to his limited range of motion, stiffness, and slowness. The animators said they had to "boil down animation to its essence" to create this character.

On the other hand, his slowness was not meant to be annoying to the audience but rather endearing. In their quest for cuteness, they developed three types of movement for Baymax: a baby, a baby with a full diaper, and a penguin chick that waddles around, curiously looking around and barely flapping its wings. They combined all these elements to create the lovable Baymax we all want to hug.

Curious: Baymax's character and some of his movements were "copied" from Totoro from Hayao Miyazaki's anime film.

Random Stats: Baymax is 182 cm tall (6 ft!) and weighs 34 kg (75 lbs). Hiro's suit makes him super strong (he can lift over 450kg/1000lbs) and even grows him 31 cm (about a foot) taller!

8. Martial Arts

To make Baymax's fighting moves look legit, the animators turned to karate! They actually went to a dojo and asked karate masters to show them moves from a kneeling position. This was because on his knees, the human body was more like Baymax's proportions.

Curious: Thanks to consultations with experienced flight specialist Jason McKinley, who previously worked on Disney's animated projects "Planes," the filmmakers made Baymax and Hiro's flights incredibly realistic and exciting.

* Rare *

9. All About Blinking

Baymax's blinks were made with old-school 2D animation, according to animation director Zach Parrish. They actually change the speed of his blinking throughout the movie, but mostly it's a standard blink. There's one special 'double blink' that means he's confused. This gives you time to think and imagine what he's feeling. It makes you part of the scene! Parrish says it's a trick actors could use, too.

10. Emotions Under Control

The animators admit they based the character and facial

expressions of the unflappable, emotionally reserved Go Go Tomago on famous actors John Wayne, Clint Eastwood, and Gary Cooper, who embodied the image of legendary cowboys of the Wild West.

Curious: Go Go Tomago's athletic physique and movement technique were inspired by professional speed skaters.

11. Fashion Flip

Wasabi was originally a very peaceful character, a kind of Zen hero with dreadlocks. But during the process of working on the film, the creators decided to slightly change his personality, realizing that such a pedant would hardly grow dreadlocks that don't like shampoo, and they cut his hair. However, the new image didn't take root. It turned out that everyone on the animation team was too used to his previous fashionable hairstyle.

Curious: It is known that "Wasabi" is not his real name, but a nickname that Fred came up with when his friend stained his pants with the same condiment.

ZOOTOPIA: UNITY IN DIVERSITY

1. Third in Line

Zootopia is the third Disney movie without any humans. The animals walk, talk, and dress like us. The other two were "Robin Hood" and "Chicken Little."

Curious: There are 64 animal species living in Zootopia. Interestingly, the creators decided not to include monkeys, due to their similarity to humans.

2. Realism First

To develop the characters and behavior of the animals, the animators visited Disney's Animal Kingdom and then Kenya, where they studied the animals' gait and behavior, color and fur.

During their trip to Kenya, the animators observed animals gathering at a watering hole, where they behaved in a civilized manner regardless of their species. This fact particularly interested the creators: the ability of animals to get along together, as well as the lifestyle of people in large cities, formed the basis of the plot.

Curious: The fur of all the animals is different, the artists considered the color and shades and made sure that the white bear's fur reflected light and the fox's fur was red at the tips.

A 45-minute documentary was made about the expedition film crew in Africa.

3. Crafting Clothes for Furry Inhabitants

New technologies allowed filmmakers to adjust the length of the fur under the costumes so that the clothes would "fit" the characters. Previously, animators had to draw fur poking out around collars by hand, one by one, as was the case, for example, with the collar of the dog Volt in the animated film "Bolt." Considering the large population of Zootopia, such a technology would have made the filming of the film incredibly laborious.

Rare

4. Scaling the Animal Kingdom

The portrayal of scale was crucial to depict a world inhabited by mammals of various sizes realistically. The filmmakers avoided the common trope of similar-sized animals, opting instead for a more true-to-life approach.

For instance, a Zootopia wildebeest, standing upright, would be as tall as an average human. To illustrate this scale, consider that it would take 24 mice stacked to reach the height of one such wildebeest, while, for a giraffe, this ratio increases to 1:97. Putting Judy and the elephant next to each other would mean that the elephant's leg would take up half of the screen, emphasizing the different sizes and how these animals coexist in the unique Zootopia ecosystem.

5. All Aboard the Zootopia Express

The vehicles are super clever about handling different-sized animals! Their train shows it off best. There are whole sections scaled to different sizes. Larger animals get normal train seats with normal-height windows. Tiny rodents travel in smaller sections with low windows just for them. Giraffes even get special cars with bubble domes to fit their huge necks!

This level of detail is awesome and makes Zootopia feel real.

6. A World of Animal Metropolises

Zootopia's all about mammals, but it's hinted that there are other cities for birds, reptiles, etc. Imagine what those places would look like!

Curious: The predators in Zootopia don't eat meat anymore. They survive on bugs and fish shipped in from the Rainforest District. Their chefs can make burgers, pizza, everything that tastes just like meat!

Craving meatless munchies? Hit up Misty's, a restaurant just for predators.

7. Different News Anchors for Different Countries

Different countries have different news anchors. In the US/Canada, it's Peter Moosebridge, an elk. Australia/New Zealand? A koala. Brazil? A jaguar. China gets a panda, and in Japan, a tanuki (a raccoon dog).

Curious: The mayor of Zootopia, Leodore Lionheart, who created the city's motto ("Zootopia, where anyone can be anything"), was inspired by Mufasa, a character from the Disney movie "The Lion King."

8. The Robin Hood Connection

The main character in Zootopia was originally supposed to be a fox. Nick's prototype was the fox from Disney's 1973 movie "Robin Hood," which also featured anthropomorphic animals. It's a great nod to a classic, don't you think?

Legendary 😆

9. A Crisis Helped the Story

Every project can hit a roadblock called "creative crisis." In November 2014, after almost a year and a half of working on Zootopia, the creators realized the concept of "Nick as the main character and Judy as a secondary character" wasn't working.

The story was more boring when told from the perspective of a jaded fox than from the perspective of the optimistic Judy, who overcomes all obstacles (including stereotypes) with her perseverance. Changing the main character made the story much better.

Curious: The original script had Nick Wilde escaping from prison after being framed for a crime he didn't commit. But in the final version, Judy Hopps teams up with Nick to investigate a missing persons case they have 48 hours to solve.

10. Blink and You'll Miss It

Movie magic is all about the details! The creators built a whole city with hidden details that make it feel familiar:

- ◇ Crosswalk signs show foxes or wolves instead of humans.
- ◇ Judy's phone has a bitten carrot logo instead of an apple.
- ◇ A giraffe holds a "Snarlbucks" coffee cup, a nod to Starbucks.

11. Breaking the Grey

Judy's eyes are purple because the animators thought her grey fur was too boring, especially for a main character. Purple represents her energetic and optimistic personality.

Curious: Judy's nose totally twitches when she's freaked out, just like a real bunny!

12. Judy Hopps is 24 Years Old

She looks younger than her age! Judy dreamed of becoming the first rabbit cop since she was 9. 15 years later, she joined the Zootopia Police Academy and got her chance.

Curious: Remember Nick's job application? He stands 4 feet tall (about 122 cm) and weighs 80 lbs (approximately 36.3 kg), which is quite hefty for a fox! And he is 32 years old.

13. Small Predator, Big Threat

The mafia boss, Mr. Big, is an arctic shrew. Director Rich Moore chose this animal because "the arctic shrew is the most vicious predator on Earth." Shrews eat three times their own weight and even kill other shrews.

Curious: Mr. Big's character is a parody of Vito Corleone from "The Godfather," with his mafia appearance and mannerisms. He's also served by the largest predators in the film: polar bears.

14. Why Does Bogo Wear Glasses?

Chief Bogo wears glasses to read in Zootopia. In an interview, the directors confirmed that this isn't just a random detail. Buffalo, like Bogo, have poor eyesight in real life. So, the creators added glasses to make the scene more realistic.

* Rare *

15. Why Zootopia's Police Force Lacks Smaller Animals

Small animals are rarely seen in the police force. Why is that?

It's all about the mafia's insidious plans! They came up with the idea that large animals in the police would be cramped in the small houses of small residents. Their brilliant solution? "Let's keep the small guys out of the police force. It'll make our secret operations easier!" And voila, their plan worked!

Curious: In the Mouse District, there's a building called the Lucky Cat Cafe - a nod to "Big Hero 6."

THE OCEAN'S CALL: MOANA

1. Between History and Myth

In "Moana", Gramma Tala mentions that their people stopped voyaging for about 1,000 years. In real history, there was a real 1,000-year "long pause" — when Polynesian voyagers stopped their long-distance journeys. No one knows the exact reason for the long pause — maybe it was due to changing wind patterns or the development of sailing technology. But according to Moana, it obviously happened because Maui stole the Heart of Te Fiti!

2. Moana Means...

The name Moana means "ocean" in many Polynesian languages, including Hawaiian and Maori.

3. Maui's Strength and Magic

Maui's main power is shapeshifting, but he can only do this if he has his magical fishhook. He's also a skilled navigator. The Gods also gave Maui incredible strength, which allowed him to pull giant islands out of the ocean, slow down the sun, and tame the wind.

Curious: When designing Maui, the team studied various athletes, football players, wrestlers, and just men with massive builds.

"You know who Maui is? He's just the greatest demigod in the whole wide Pacific!" – Maui, being totally modest tells Moana

4. A Tattoo with a Soul

Mini Maui is a living, intelligent, and sentient tattoo on the demigod Maui's body and his best friend. He embodies the best qualities that Maui himself lacks. Honest and fair, he makes his irresponsible and sometimes selfish host make the right choice in difficult situations.

Curious: Although the film is mostly computer-animated, Mini Maui was created traditionally – hand-drawn.

During the film's creation, the animation team specifically asked to add scenes with Mini Maui for the opportunity to work with animation legend Eric Goldberg.

5. Tamatoa is David Bowie as a Crab 🦀

"Moana" fans claim that the song Shiny, performed by the giant crab Tamatoa, was written by the creators inspired by the work of David Bowie. This is a very logical theory, especially considering that Tamatoa's pupils, like those of the great musician, are different sizes.

RAYA AND THE LAST DRAGON

1. Southeast Asia on Screen

Raya and the Last Dragon is a fast-paced adventure with stunning visuals and an amazing soundtrack. The filmmakers even took a research trip to Thailand, Vietnam, Cambodia, and the Philippines to create the film's beautiful landscapes.

Curious: Raya is the 13th Disney princess and the first Southeast Asian Disney princess!

Legendary 😃

2. Magical Blue Friends

If you've seen Raya and the Last Dragon, you might have noticed some similarities between Sisu and Genie from Aladdin. These two magical creatures are not only similar in appearance, but they also have a lot in common in terms of character and destiny.

◇ **Color:** Sisu and Genie are both blue, which symbolizes wisdom, magic, and power.

◇ **Ancient Origins:** Both characters were awakened after a long sleep - Sisu slept for 500 years, and Genie was trapped in a lamp for 10,000 years.

◇ **Introduction to Modernity:** Sisu and Genie are both curious about the modern world, its technology, and its culture.

◇ **Sense of Humor:** Both characters can joke and make people laugh.

◇ **Friendliness and Compassion:** Sisu and Genie are always ready to help those in need.

◇ **Love of Freedom:** Both characters value freedom and do not tolerate restrictions.

- ⋄ **Wisdom:** Sisu and Genie possess deep knowledge and life experience.

> **Funny Fact:** Sisu and Genie talking about tech: "So, can this 'internet' get me a new lamp?"

3. Where Does Sisu Get Her Strength? The Finnish Roots of the Dragon's Name

Did you realize that "Sisu," the dragon's name in "Raya and the Last Dragon," wasn't just whimsically chosen by Disney? It actually derives from a Finnish term that's loaded with depth and resilience. "Sisu" in Finnish culture represents a unique mix of grit, resolve, endurance, and the ability to face challenges with thoughtful action. It's about maintaining courage consistently, not just in fleeting moments.

Picture yourself braving a massive snowstorm, choosing to push forward not merely because it's possible, but because it feels fundamentally right. That's the essence of "sisu." This concept perfectly encapsulates Sisu the dragon. She's more than brave and optimistic; she's indomitable, demonstrating what it means to persevere against all odds.

Disney masterfully integrates rich cultural values into its characters, making them meaningful on a global scale. Sisu isn't only magical; she represents a significant cultural principle, inspiring us with the value of resilience and the vital need to keep moving forward, no matter the challenges ahead.

Do you have an example of real "sisu"?

INTERESTING STORY: ENCANTO

1. Colombian Cultural Fiesta in 'Encanto'

"Encanto" is a vibrant celebration of Colombian culture, music, and landscapes. The creators made sure everything in the film, from the dance moves to the scenery, is authentically Colombian.

Curious: The film's magical realism is inspired by Latin American literature, blending magic with real-world settings.

2. The Magic of Casita

The Madrigal family's house, Casita, is not just a building; it's almost like a member of the family! This magical house is alive with personality. It greets family members, moves to the rhythm of the music, and even helps out with daily chores. Imagine living in a house that not only dances with you but also cleans up your room!

Curious: Casita's ability to interact with the Madrigal family not only provides comic relief and visual delight but also symbolizes the family's deep connection to their heritage. The house's movements and reactions are carefully animated to reflect its personality and role in the story, showcasing the innovative animation techniques used in "Encanto."

> **Funny Fact:** Who needs a cleaning robot when your house can boogie the dust away?

3. Your Personality, Your Dance Style

Each character dances in a style that reflects their personality. Luisa's movements are choreographed to Reggaeton, aligning with her strength and power. Mirabel, in contrast, showcases her adaptability: she dances to Cali Salsa when alone, a style noted for its energy and complexity and adapts to other styles when with family, underscoring her role as the empathetic connector in the Madrigal family.

4. The Madrigal Family's Magic in Fashion!

Let's take a magical wardrobe tour with the Madrigal family from "Encanto"! Each member's clothes are like a fun clue to their cool powers. ✺

Juileta's apron is an adorned with plant images to show off her unique talent of healing through her delicious dishes.

Pepa's dress and sun-shaped earrings mirror her ability to change the weather.

Bruno rocks a poncho with hourglass designs, a stylish nod to his gift of seeing into the future.

Isabela's dress is a floral fantasy! It's covered in flowers, showcasing her amazing ability to make plants and flowers bloom.

Luisa's skirt is no less than a fashion statement of strength, with weights symbolizing her incredible physical power. It's like her own superhero costume!

Dolores' outfit is a nod to her super-hearing, with soundwave patterns.

Antonio's top is a tribute to his ability to talk to animals, with various animal motifs.

Mirabel has a special pink butterfly on her shoulder, representing both her family and their magical house, Casita. It's like a symbol of her connection to her family's legacy.

So, as you dive back into the colorful world of "Encanto," keep an eye out for these fantastic fashion details that add an extra layer of magic to the Madrigal family's story.

5. Luisa's Muscle Power

Did you know there was a bit of a tug-of-war behind the scenes of "Encanto" about Luisa's look? Dylan Ekren, the character designer, spilled the beans on social media. He shared that convincing Disney Animation to give Luisa a muscular build was no easy feat. Ekren tweeted about wanting to make it fit the style and really make sense for Luisa's character. And guess what? He's super proud of how she turned out!

In the Disney world, where female characters often lean towards the slim and petite side, Luisa stands out with her muscles, showing off her strength in a cool and refreshing way.

6. Bruno's Sad Room

The magical house Casita is vibrant and full of life, except in Bruno's room, where there's a noticeable absence of magic. This lack of energy in Bruno's space symbolizes his estrangement from the family and his misunderstood nature. The stark contrast between the lively areas of Casita and the stillness of Bruno's room visually represents his isolation within the family.

* Rare *

7. Bruno's Superstitions

In the movie "Encanto," there's a character named Bruno who can see the future. But despite his amazing gift, he does a lot of superstitious things to avoid bad luck. Bruno knocks on wood to ward off bad fortune, throws salt over his shoulder, and avoids stepping on cracks.

It seems these habits developed because his family always considered his predictions a source of trouble.

BONUS SECTION: HIDDEN DISNEY TREASURES

Welcome to the bonus section, where I've collected some unique and interesting facts about the Disney world I just couldn't leave out!

1. Scrooge's Money Sea 💰

In "DuckTales," Scrooge's fortune is revealed. According to Scrooge's accountant Fenton, Scrooge's fortune is $987 trillion, 520 billion, and 36 cents.

Curious: Nobody knows how old Scrooge is for sure, but he thinks he's still in his prime. The comics, though, say his birthday is Dec 24, 1867.

2. Personal Matters 🐱

Even kittens have their own little secrets that animation masters love to subtly weave into the story. For example, in the cartoon "Pinocchio," the cat Figaro boasts his own litter box instead of a potty. Apparently, even cartoon cats have standards.

3. Dumbo Had a Chance to Be on the Cover of Time

When Disney's fifth animated film was released in the summer of 1941, it was praised by critics and audiences alike. By the beginning of the Christmas holidays, the creators had managed to earn almost $2.5 million on it. Time Magazine almost put Dumbo on the cover for Dec 29, 1941...until the attack on Pearl Harbor happened. Nevertheless, Dumbo was featured in the "Cinema" section.

* Rare *

4. The Famous Spaghetti and Kiss Moment with Lady and the Tramp Could Have Been Cut

Today, this episode is one of the most famous and parodied in the film industry. However, Walt Disney was against this cozy scene. Although he wanted the characters to have human emotions, he considered such behavior of dogs to be completely implausible. Animals that share food with each other cannot be graceful. In the end, animator Frank Thomas developed a rough version of the scene that convinced Disney.

5. Worldwide Transformations of the Famous M🐭use

While Mickey Mouse seems to be a universally known character, not everyone recognizes him by that name. If you mention him in China, no one will understand you, there the mouse is called "Mi Lao Shu." And in Spain - "El Raton Mickey Mouse," in Indonesia - "Mickey Mikus," in Finland - "Mikki Hihi." Everything is clear: the word "mouse" sounds different in another language. But why Mickey Mouse becomes "Topolino" in Italy is a more confusing question!

6. Mickey for President: A Quirky American Tradition

Get this: Mickey Mouse regularly gets votes in US elections! About 1% of voters write in Mickey's name every year, and in 2008, that number jumped to 5%. This quirky tradition shows voter dissatisfaction with the candidates and provides a humorous way to express protest.

> **Funny Fact:** Maybe candidates should start wearing red shorts and big yellow shoes to increase their chances! 👀

7. Donald Duck: Protest Viking Style

Like Mickey in the US, Donald is all over politics in Scandinavia, but...angrier! Americans use Mickey to joke about bad candidates, but in Finland and Sweden, Donald is the serious protest vote. Dissatisfied voters write his name on ballots, suggesting that a cartoon character with occasional anger issues might seem preferable to the real contenders.

8. Modern Footwear in a Medieval World ✨ 👟

"Wish" is set in the 1200s, but Asha's shoes look straight-up modern, a clever nod from the creators to show she's ahead of her time. Interestingly, her shoes take inspiration from Princess Diana's iconic wedding slippers. This detail is like a cool Easter egg linking past and present, emphasizing Asha's progressive nature.

★ Rare ★

9. Spot Overload!

In "101 Dalmatians," a whopping 6,469,952 spots are on display! That's no surprise considering Pongo has 72 spots, Perdita has 68, and each puppy has 32.

10. Sleeping Beauty: The Queen of Silence

Despite the movie being all about her, Aurora only has 18 minutes of screen time in total. And she's pretty quiet: she doesn't speak at all in the second half of the movie! But Aurora makes up for her silence with beautiful vocals: her singing voice was provided by professional opera singer Mary Costa!

Curious: While Aurora is the most silent Disney princess (with only 18 lines in the movie), the real record-holder is Dumbo. He's the only main character in a Disney animated film who doesn't say a single word!

11. Notre Dame's Stone Secrets

In "The Hunchback of Notre Dame," the cathedral plays more than just a backdrop – it's a real character! One of the most memorable details of the cathedral is its gargoyles – the stone monsters that decorate its facade. In the movie, they come to life, becoming Quasimodo's friends and protectors.

The main gargoyles are Victor, Hugo, and Laverne. They're hilarious, always there to cheer Quasi up, and help him out when things get rough.

Curious: Victor and Hugo seem to be named after Victor Hugo, the author of The Hunchback of Notre Dame, while Laverne was named after Laverne Andrews of the 1940s singing group.

12. Belle and Aladdin's Carpet in 'The Hunchback of Notre Dame'

In a "Hunchback of Notre Dame" cameo, Belle from "Beauty and the Beast" makes an appearance!

Keep your eyes peeled: when Quasimodo sings "Out There," you can spot Belle wandering the streets of Paris, still nose-deep in a book. Her presence makes sense since she also lives in France. And if you look even closer, you can see a man shaking out Aladdin's magic carpet in the same scene!

DEAR DISNEY EXPLORERS

Thank you for embarking on this magical journey through the "Interesting Facts about the World of Disney" with me. Your choice to dive into this book means the world, and I am deeply thankful.

I hope our adventure has sparked even more curiosity and love for the enchanting universe Disney has created. If this book has brought a little more magic into your life, I'd be thrilled to hear your thoughts. Your feedback is a treasure, more valuable than any genie's lamp. 😊

Don't let the magic end here. Follow my Author Page 🔖 on Amazon to discover new and exciting worlds, perhaps not only of Disney. Whether it's the depths of space or the mysteries of magic, our adventure continues.

"Remember, all our dreams can come true if we have the courage to pursue them." – Walt Disney

✨ 🔮 ✨

With magical wishes,

Max Galaxy

Explore More Magic

As I work on my next books, I invite you to explore two enchanting titles about the Wizarding World, penned by my good friend Newt Flamel:

①

Harry Potter Spellbook: The Unofficial Illustrated Guide to Wizard Training.

Dive into the intricacies of magical incantations and the histories behind them—a must-have for any budding wizard.

②

Harry Potter Magic Facts: The Unofficial Illustrated Book to Wizard Fun.

Discover lesser-known facts and secrets that illuminate corners of the wizarding world even the most devout fans might not know.

The Next Chapter in Magic...

Make sure to subscribe to stay updated on upcoming releases that promise to enchant and delight.

Printed in Great Britain
by Amazon